Between the easy-to-read stories and observations, Jay delivers the kind of insight that helps give purpose to our time on earth. Keep reading and be ready to experience the abundant life Jesus promises.

Josh McDowell
author of *More Than a Carpenter*
and *The New Evidence That Demands a Verdict*

I love *What If God Wrote Your Bucket List?* As I've gotten older, I've realized that life is all about moving from success to significance to surrender. So rather than living the rest of our lives completely on our own agenda, let's think about what God's agenda might be for us. With an enjoyable, non-preachy approach, Jay Payleitner gently challenges us to get out of our own way. A great read and a great blessing.

Ken Blanchard
coauthor of *The New One Minute Manager*
and *Lead Like Jesus*

When you're as old as I am, you need to keep your bucket list short and doable. I've just junked the bucket list I had and have found a much better one in Jay's book. This isn't one of those books that make you feel guilty about things you probably can't do. It's a practical, biblical, grace-filled, and fun way to live out your walk with Christ. Read this book and you, with me, will rise up and call Jay blessed. It might even change your life.

Steve Brown
radio broadcaster, seminary professor,
and author of *Three Free Sins: God's Not Mad at You*

Are you working your plan? Or God's plan? *What If God Wrote Your Bucket List?* will make you smile and think, and it will equip you for your best plan going forward.

Bob Tiede
director of global operation leadership development, CRU

What If God Wrote Your Bucket List? is a deep and rich treasure, at once thoughtful and whimsical. Jay brings the finer gold of the Christian life to light in this remarkable read.

Brannon J. Marshall
director of church engagement, Awana International

My friend Jay Payleitner has given you and me a very special gift. *What If God Wrote Your Bucket List?* is more than an extraordinary book—it is energizing and thought provoking for anyone wanting to seriously look at the last third of their life as potentially more impactful and dynamic than all their previous years. It's not just to be read but also to be used as a life-planning tool for all who seriously want to finish well.

Chuck Stecker
president and founder,
A Chosen Generation & the Center for InterGenerational Ministry

Whether or not you have a bucket list, God has one for you. And it's a doozy. Jay's book will remind you of the many exciting adventures that can be found within even the most ordinary pursuits in our lives. Make reading this book part of your bucket list.

Leary Gates
president, the National Coalition of Ministries to Men

Working in politics and public policy for more than 20 years, I know it's not always easy to focus on the goals God would have us pursue rather than the ones the world tells us are most important. That's why I was personally delighted to see this book from Jay Payleitner, who in 52 concise and story-telling chapters gives us encouragement to seek first the kingdom of God.

Genevieve Wood
The Heritage Foundation

It's rare to come across someone who can get you to stop and think about serious personal application while keeping you smiling and chuckling at the same time. Payleitner has hit that mark for any generation with this book— a great read.

Brandon Aldridge
director of ministry services, Men's Ministry Catalyst

For a long time I've been wanting to write a book about making a spiritual bucket list. Well, my friend Jay Payleitner has beaten me to it and has done a much better job than I could have. If you have ever wondered how to align your choices in life with God's will, this is the book for you.

Edward Grinnan
editor in chief, Guideposts Publications

WHAT IF
GOD
WROTE YOUR
BUCKET
LIST?

JAY PAYLEITNER

HARVEST HOUSE PUBLISHERS
EUGENE, OREGON

Cover by Lucas Art and Design, Jenison, Michigan

Cover photo © PicsFive / Masterfile

Published in association with the literary agency of the Steve Laube Agency, LLC, 5025 N. Central Ave., #635, Phoenix, Arizona, 85012.

WHAT IF GOD WROTE YOUR BUCKET LIST?

Copyright © 2015 Jay Payleitner
Published by Harvest House Publishers
Eugene, Oregon 97402
www.harvesthousepublishers.com

Library of Congress Cataloging-in-Publication Data
    Payleitner, Jay K.
    What if God wrote your bucket list? / Jay Payleitner.
        pages cm
    ISBN 978-0-7369-6270-4 (pbk.)
    ISBN 978-0-7369-6271-1 (eBook)
    1. Christian life. I. Title.
    BV4501.3.P395 2015
    248.4—dc23

                                                      2015013610

Printed in the United States of America

15 16 17 18 19 20 21 22 23 / BP-CD / 10 9 8 7 6 5 4 3 2 1

To Paul Gossard,
who knows the way

Acknowledgments

For 25 years, I've been given specific assignments and deadlines to seek truth, know truth, present truth, and draw individuals to the truth. In every media imaginable. Print, radio, television, social media, direct mail, video walls, books, periodicals, and public speaking. Even T-shirts, posters, and distributing literature on street corners in Moscow. That's what happens when you establish yourself as a freelance writer/producer/speaker in the Christian marketplace.

Let me share a few career highlights. Writing the first print ad for Jerry Jenkins and Tim LaHaye's megaselling Left Behind series. Recording Josh McDowell speaking with a guard in a Soviet-era prison. Being a guest on *Focus on the Family*. Producing broadcasts featuring Bill Bright, Zig Ziglar, Chuck Colson, Dennis Rainey, Luis Palau, TobyMac, and many other respected Christian communicators. Speaking on behalf of Iron Sharpens Iron, AWANA, MOPS, the National Center for Fathering, and scores of local churches and regional ministries.

I am humbly grateful to the leadership and media teams of all those ministries and many others. Your integrity, passion, and commitment to truth and excellence have forever impacted my life and most assuredly can be found in the pages of this book.

Thank you to my agent and dear friend, Dan Balow. And to the team at Harvest House, especially my patient editor, Gene Skinner. I appreciate your TLC more than you know.

To my growing family—Rita, Alec, Lindsay, Randall, Rachel, Max, Megan, Isaac, Kaitlin, Rae Anne, Judah, Jackson, and Emerson—you inspire and motivate me. I love you all.

And to my Savior, Jesus, who went to the cross for each and every one of us. Without your perfect love, none of this makes any sense.

Contents

Foreword

by Josh D. McDowell

Our Creator is in the business of creating order out of chaos. God uses lists to help us order our lives and learn more about him. He used a seven-day plan to create the universe. He gave Moses a list on Mount Sinai—the Ten Commandments. Jesus provided a wonderfully useful list of eternal values, the Beatitudes, as a code of ethics for those who would follow him. The nine fruit of the Spirit are listed in Galatians as virtues God develops in every believer. God doesn't want us to obsess about making lists or panic about checking off dozens of specific tasks before we die, but lists can be very handy.

My list-making goes way back. During my first year in college, I drafted a multi-point strategic plan for the next 25 years of my life. It wasn't called a bucket list back then, but my goals were dead serious. I mapped out 50 six-month periods with clear objectives and concrete plans for the next quarter century. My strategic plan ended with me being elected governor of Michigan.

The first step was running for and being elected freshman class president. Check. In the next few months, I tackled a few more objectives. Check, check, and check. The next major item of my strategic plan was a required yearlong research project. I knew it had to be a controversial topic with significant historical, cultural, and legal implications, and I had to knock it out of the park. I also knew that if I was going to invest a year of my life, it would need to be a topic for which I had a personal passion and something to prove.

Those who have heard my testimony won't be surprised to hear the topic I chose for that term paper. At the time, I was still struggling with my mother's death and my father's alcoholism. Looking for answers, I had turned briefly to religion but found it shallow, phony, and foolish. That's when I told my English professor I was going to do a serious historical study that would—once and for all—refute Christianity as nothing but meaningless fables.

My months of research uncovered a list of 119 separate events and situations I would have to explain away before I could honestly and intellectually reject Jesus Christ. As I studied, my carefully constructed strategic plan started to derail, and the research led me to the place we all need to be—at the foot of the cross, acknowledging our sin and asking God to forgive us and clean up our lives.

Since then, my strategic plan has been dedicated to answering God's call. You might think the plan would be quite complex. But it really isn't. You might even call it my "three-point bucket list." In more than 50 years, I've given thousands of talks and written thousands of pages, and it all comes down to these three points: "Get to heaven. Take as many people with me as possible. Enjoy every moment."

This three-point plan still motivates me in all I do. But I can also certainly see how 14 words don't exactly fill a book. That's why I'm glad my friend Jay Payleitner has taken on the challenge of hanging meat on that skeleton. Between the easy-to-read stories and observations, Jay delivers the kind of insight that helps give purpose to our time on earth. I believe any reader who opens their heart and mind to these 52 chapters will discover they are right in line with God's will for their lives. So keep reading. And be ready to experience the abundant life Jesus promises in John 10:10 when he says, "I have come that they may have life, and have it to the full."

Got a Bucket List?

You know the concept, right? Otherwise you wouldn't have picked up this book.

Briefly defined. A bucket list is quite literally a list—written down or mulled over in your mind—of things you want to do before you kick the bucket.

The term was actually little known until the 2007 movie directed by Rob Reiner and starring Jack Nicholson and Morgan Freeman. If you haven't seen *The Bucket List*, I recommend it. The veteran actors portray Edward and Carter, older gentlemen from differing backgrounds sharing a hospital room, undergoing chemo treatments, and revealing regrets of two lives unfulfilled. Diagnosed with terminal cancer—and against their doctor's advice—they set off on a breathtaking trip around the world to cross off items from a handwritten checklist of things to do before they die. Edward and Carter make some bad choices and some good ones. And they ask spiritual questions we all need to ask.

But this book is not about their bucket list. It's about yours.

More specifically, it's about the bucket list you might compose if you were totally in sync with how God wants you to live your life. Now, you might think the all-powerful Creator of the universe would have some pretty outrageous goals for each one of us. And he does. His goals for us take a lifetime to achieve. But at first glance, God's bucket list for you may not seem quite as spectacular as a conventional one.

God's recommendations for your bucket list probably won't include destinations and extravaganzas that make headlines or wow your friends. But you will find decisions, truths, and insights that are truly transformational.

Instead of moving to a more upscale neighborhood, your new goal may be to love your current neighbor.

Instead of dining with the hottest Hollywood celebrities, your new goal may be to break bread with someone who's down on their luck and needs a good meal.

Instead of convincing the city council to erect a statue of your likeness in the town square, your new goal might be to establish a home with a solid foundation for your family.

God's bucket list for your life probably includes fewer things to do and more things to embrace. Things to appreciate. To choose. And sometimes to let go.

Want to know something? If these are on your personal bucket list, I hope you *do* climb Mount Everest, run with the bulls in Spain, sleep in an igloo, get invited to the White House, or collect Starbucks mugs from all 50 states. Sounds like fun.

But no matter what, don't miss these 52 things God would probably write on your bucket list. When you finally look back at all you have achieved, don't be surprised if God's plan for your life turns out to be a gazillion times more soul satisfying than anything you could possibly dream for yourself.

> *In the end, life can't be about checking off items on a*
> *bucket list. It has to be about pouring out your bucket*
> *on behalf of neighbors, lovers, strangers, and friends.*
>
> JAY PAYLEITNER

Set Goals—but Not in Concrete

Digging through some old papers, I ran across a list of personal goals I had written almost two decades ago. Not a bucket list for my life, but goals for a specific calendar year. I will not share the contents of that list here. After all, they were my goals, not yours. But I will confirm that some were very specific. Others were more of an attitude adjustment. Some were one-time events. Some were achieved. Others were not. And some are still ongoing personal projects.

Clearly, I had taken the task seriously. All the goals had long-term relevance and real-life application. I didn't write, "Score more than 250,000 points in Donkey Kong," or "Videotape and catalog every episode of *Saved by the Bell*." Most of the goals could fall into one of four categories: spiritual growth, personal relationships, financial planning, and career advancement.

None of the goals were as simplistic as "Be happier," although checking off one of those goals would have provided a satisfying moment. As I recall, I pulled out the list a few times that year but didn't post it on the wall or make a personal pledge to review it weekly. Actually, this is the first time I've told anyone about the list. Now tucked in a file folder, the list still challenges me and perhaps mocks me just a little.

On the one hand, every personal trainer or management consultant in the world extols the virtue of goal setting. Goals help you keep your eyes on the prize. Goals can drag you out of bed in the morning.

On the other hand, your goals for your life are not nearly as important as God's goals for your life. In other words, please don't be surprised if all your careful planning and goal setting gets set aside by the master planner himself. The Bible reminds us, "We can make our plans, but the LORD determines our steps" (Proverbs 16:9 NLT). That idea is confirmed again and again in Scripture.

The Tower of Babel was planned as a monument to the people themselves. As a result, God confused their language, and the tower was never completed.

In the parable of the rich fool, Jesus tells the story of a wealthy farmer who planned to build bigger barns to hold his abundant crops. That very night the farmer died in his sleep.

The night Jesus is betrayed by Judas, Peter attacks a soldier, cutting off his ear. Jesus heals the soldier and allows himself to be arrested without further incident, knowing that his bigger purpose was to fulfill God's plan.

So what's your plan? What goals do you have for the weekend or the year or your life? Goals are good. Specific goals are even better. Don't just write down, "Work out more." Commit to specific times and places. Don't just write, "Join a Bible study." Round up some friends and set a weekly agenda. Don't just say, "Get my degree." Make an appointment with a college admissions counselor.

But don't be surprised if on your way to doing something good and admirable, God provides you with a surprising opportunity to do something great and amazing.

Checking the List

As you discern God's bucket list for your life and set personal goals, be specific. Being wishy-washy is never good. Be bold. Forge ahead. Give yourself deadlines and five-year plans. Take risks.

Challenge authority. Build consensus. Maintain high expectations. But don't forget also to expect the unexpected. Never stop praying. Never stop pursuing God's will. You might actually hear direct instructions from heaven, such as "Noah, build a boat," "Abraham, put down that knife," "Joseph, marry that pregnant girl," or "Peter, get out of the boat and walk on the water." God often uses the unexpected to get your attention, drive home a lesson, and do his best work in you and through you.

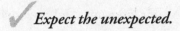 *Expect the unexpected.*

Drive Through the Storm

When I was ten, my family took a camping trip from the Chicago suburbs to New Mexico and back. I'm not sure about our exact return route, the miles we traveled each day, or the location of the campgrounds we stayed in, but I do remember this. The first day started beautifully, but as we traveled east, we ended up driving through a fierce thunderstorm. On the other side of the storm, we quickly set up camp on dry ground and cooked a campfire dinner as the sun was setting. Overnight, the rains caught up with us, pounding our six-man tent. We slept little, and in the morning we packed up our gear in the mud.

Over the next four days, we repeated the same pattern. Drive through the storm. Find a campground. Pitch a damp tent. Listen to the thunder and hope the tent doesn't leak. Pack up in the mud. Hit the road.

My parents were troopers about the whole thing, and that attitude seemed to rub off on us kids. I remember a sense of adventure and inevitability about the events of the coming day.

"There's the storm line," my dad would say.

"Should we stop now or try to get ahead of it?" Mom would ask.

Moments later, the windshield wipers would come on, and we'd be surrounded with lightning bolts for the next hour or so.

Oddly enough, surviving that storm—five times—was not the most significant memory of that trip. One of those muddy mornings happened to be a Sunday, and my parents were determined to find a worthwhile church service for us to attend. (Remember, this was before Google Maps and cell phones.) We broke camp, checked our maps, got off the main highway, asked around, and finally made it to what looked like a nice little church…just as the last cars were leaving the parking lot after the last service of the day.

Still, the six of us piled out of the station wagon, and Dad led us into the surprisingly empty chapel. Without saying much, Dad entered a pew, and we joined him in a few quiet moments of reflection and prayer. Reflecting on that scenario, I am sure my parents never knew the magnitude of the lesson they had provided for this ten-year-old boy. We were not in that building out of necessity. No one was taking attendance. We were not there to listen to a pastor or show off our Sunday-go-to-meeting clothes. (After all, what we wore was slightly damp and rumpled.) We were there because God is God. And we need to be intentional about spending time with him.

Yes, of course, we can talk to God anytime. He's everywhere. We don't have to be in a building with a cross on the steeple and wooden pews. But for several days we had been surrounded by clear reminders of God's power and presence. Whether they knew it or not, my mom and dad were making a statement to their four children. And thanking God for his ongoing provision.

Minutes later we were on the road and heading into another storm front. But that was a turning point for me. For the rest of my life, I had a radically different perspective on God and how humans need to relate to him. The Creator of the universe surely appreciates well-delivered sermons, worshipful hymns, polished shoes, and a full collection plate. But the item he wants most on our bucket list is a humble acknowledgment that we can't do life without him. Through sunny days and stormy nights, he is our sole provider, protector, and guide.

Checking the List

Storms are coming. And God allows the rain to fall on everyone—those who choose to follow him and those who don't. The best place to be in a storm is not on a highway or in a tent. The best place to be is in a house with a firm foundation. Matthew 7:25 confirms, "The rain came down, the streams rose, and the winds blew and beat against that house; yet it did not fall, because it had its foundation on the rock."

Amazingly, if you have put your faith and trust in Jesus, you should occasionally *choose* to drive into the storm. You need not worry. You will be safe. Your life will stand as a witness to those who have mistakenly built their foundation on something other than Jesus the rock.

 Build a foundation that withstands the storms.

Become like Little Children

O ur fourth son, Isaac, always had a slightly healthier imagination than the rest of our crew. As a preschooler, he spent a season of his life experimenting with his designated superhero powers. More than once, Isaac was observed tying a pillowcase around his neck, diving off our coffee table, and wondering why "the darn cape didn't work." (By our fourth male child, we didn't spend a lot of time panicking about boys standing on furniture.)

Isaac was not a cartoon junkie. But like his dad, he did appreciate the finer points of how science was allowed to go slightly askew when Wile E. Coyote, Bugs Bunny, and other Warner Brothers characters were involved. For instance, a character squashed by a falling anvil will walk away from the scene looking and sounding like an accordion. That's simple cartoon physics. Likewise, when stepping off a cliff, gravity doesn't apply until the individual suspended in space realizes he is no longer on solid ground. Cartoon physics also permits two-dimensional black circular holes to be picked up and moved to alternate locations. And of course, when an individual is propelled with sufficient force through a solid wall, door, or billboard, they leave behind a perfect outline of their body, including ears, whiskers, and anything they were carrying. Animators sometimes call such a character-shaped hole an impact silhouette.

Isaac was at the height of his quest to test the veracity of cartoon physics the summer he turned four years old. He was out helping his mom plant the small plot of land we called our garden, and Rita watched as her curious son's attention turned to the garden rake they had just used to loosen the soil. He studied the six-foot rake for several seconds, and then before she knew it, Isaac had turned it over—teeth side up—and stepped on it. Of course, the wooden handle sprang up off the ground and clunked him in the forehead. Delighted, Isaac shouted, "It worked! It worked!"

A four-year-old boy steps out in faith (on a garden rake) and responds with joy. That's something an adult would never do intentionally. That's because we're so smart. We already think we have all the answers. But the truth is, we don't.

Scientists desperately want to know how the universe began. They can't know, so they speculate. As enlightened adults, our sense of justice compels us to agonize over the question of why illness or tragedy hits one family and not another. And since we can't describe heaven, many of us choose not to believe at all.

The Bible tells us that at some point in our life, we need to be like a child who takes a step of faith. It's a basic bucket-list assignment. To be curious. Wide-eyed. Dependent. Trusting. That's what Jesus meant when he said, "Truly I tell you, unless you change and become like little children, you will never enter the kingdom of heaven" (Matthew 18:3).

Afterward, once you have secured your citizenship in heaven, you can begin to ask those tougher questions. When you ask about the universe, God will reveal his majesty in the stars—stars he hung in place. When illness and tragedy strike and you look for justice, he will give you comfort in his promise, "'He will wipe every tear from their eyes. There will be no more death' or mourning or crying or pain, for the old order of things has passed away" (Revelation 21:4). If you wonder what heaven is like, he will give you a glimpse of glory when you are in fellowship with other believers or loved by your friends or family. Again,

God's clear answers to life's greatest puzzles may sound like nonsense to those who don't believe in God. On the other hand, mature believers will ask, hear, and understand.

When Bible scholars consider the issue of childlike faith, they agree. It's not being childish or ignorant or naive. Childlike faith means you finally see God as a trustworthy heavenly Father.

When new believers begin to mature in Christ, 1 Corinthians 13:11 applies: "When I was a child, I talked like a child, I thought like a child, I reasoned like a child. When I became a man, I put the ways of childhood behind me."

But once in a while—when you're tired or beaten up, or when doubt creeps in—don't hesitate to come back to your heavenly Father and say, "Let me rest in you."

Checking the List

It's soul-satisfying to know that we can call on God the Father anytime. And because we know him and he loves us, his communication will be clear. Even if we don't get all the nuances. "Because we are his children, God has sent the Spirit of his Son into our hearts, prompting us to call out, 'Abba, Father'" (Galatians 4:6).

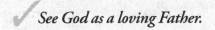 *See God as a loving Father.*

Be Last in Line

When I was in college, I made this declaration more than once: "I will never live in a house with a white picket fence."

That was my way of taking a stand against a life of meaningless existence. Sure, I knew I'd probably get married and have one or two kids. But a house in suburbia? With a picket fence? And a minivan? Not a chance. I was better than that. I was going to do great things. Mowing a lawn or cleaning gutters would just get in the way.

For the record, I have never owned or erected a white picket fence. However, at the second house we owned, I came home from work one day to an image that could have rocked my world. My neighbor had installed a lovely and sturdy white picket fence—which meant the entire north side of my property now stood in mocking defiance of the personal pledge I had made ten years earlier.

But you know what? It was not a big deal. I looked at that fence and laughed. By that time, I had three kids and had surrendered to the conformity and wonder of suburban life. (Including owning a minivan.)

Seeing that fence helped me realize who I was and what my life had become. I had not sold out. I had not turned my back on a freethinking, rebellious, countercultural lifestyle. Instead, I had found something better.

The desire to do great things was still there. But when I looked at my family, I realized that my dedication to serving them was as great as any human endeavor could be.

In one of the most amusing scenes in the Bible, all 12 disciples are walking along behind Jesus, arguing about which of them is the greatest. As recorded in Mark 9, while the group of men travel from Galilee to Capernaum, Jesus shares some pretty amazing stuff, even describing his inevitable betrayal, death, and resurrection. But the disciples are barely listening. They don't get it. Instead, each of them has been staking claim to the head of the line when it comes to Jesus's sidekicks.

Even though he knows their every thought, Jesus asks, "What were you arguing about on the road?" They get real quiet. Then Jesus delivers this stunner: "Anyone who wants to be first must be the very last, and the servant of all." The 12 disciples have been acting like children, and Jesus has just pointed it out. To emphasize the point, he picks up a little kid who happens to be hanging around, and he adds, "Whoever welcomes one of these little children in my name welcomes me" (Mark 9:37). Once again, Jesus turns conventional wisdom upside down.

Want to do great things? Me too. Let's start with serving our families—including our kids, spouse, parents, siblings, nieces, and nephews. Then we can move on to serving our neighbors and the rest of the planet.

Live as a servant to all, and you'll not only feel great, you'll be great.

Checking the List

To be great in the eyes of the world pretty much involves being first. First to reach the mountaintop. First at the box office. First in rushing yards or home runs. First in line at the bank. First place in whatever race you're running.

But true greatness comes when you let others go ahead of you. Yes, we should absolutely strive for excellence. God wants us to use our gifts and give our best efforts in all we do. But when glory comes, give it away, and you can check one more item off that bucket list. Put others ahead of yourself. Actually, put *everyone* ahead of yourself. Which makes you last. But that's okay, because in God's economy, "The last will be first, and the first will be last" (Matthew 20:16).

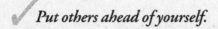 *Put others ahead of yourself.*

Reconsider Rules Carved in Stone

Since the dawn of creation, mankind has been on a quest for the meaning of life. And that's a good thing. Seeking answers to the core questions of who we are, why we're here, and how to make the most of our lives is a noble and worthwhile endeavor.

But what if the answers already came and we cast them aside? What if Moses actually did talk to a burning bush and carry two stone tablets containing ten perfect laws down from Mount Sinai? If God himself carved those ten rules for life and we missed it, then all we have left to guide us is our own limited and flawed perspective and a confusing array of half-truths and outright lies offered by the world.

Does that scare you? It should. But it shouldn't surprise us. We humans love to flaunt our independence. "Rules from God?" we ask. "Sure, he might exist," we'll say, but we don't really want him interfering in our everyday lives with a set of antiquated rules. Rules are limiting. Rules take the fun out of life. Who wants to live inside a set of arbitrary and hard-to-understand boundaries?

Those are valid points—if we're talking about man-made rules. But we're still asking, "What if?" When God makes rules, there must be a reason, and the reason would probably be to protect us and provide for us, which would be true even if we couldn't clearly see the long-term, big-picture plan he has mapped out.

So when it comes to items God would include on your bucket list, doesn't it make sense to at least take a closer look at a list of rules he has already clearly provided? We certainly don't want to miss the obvious. So how about looking at the Ten Commandments as a gift from a loving Father? Maybe then we would realize those rules were not limiting, but freeing.

You've heard the analogy before. When a little toddler reaches for the stove, the loving parents says, "No! Hot!" and might even slap the little hand about to be burned. The loving parent puts a fence around a swimming pool, insists the kids wear their seat belts, and enforces curfews. Often, limits equal love. Again, what if the Ten Commandments create a master grid for a life of satisfaction?

When the Ten Commandments were first introduced to the world, the crowd waiting at the bottom of Mount Sinai were initially impressed, but it didn't last. As Moses was having a close encounter with the Creator of the universe, the Israelites were melting their jewelry into a golden calf. Theologians suggest they needed to worship something they could see and touch. Apparently a burning bush and voices thundering from the sky weren't enough.

Here in the twenty-first century, we're way too sophisticated and intellectual to listen to millennia-old rules.

Maybe that explains why the Ten Commandments don't get much attention these days. Unless some alleged religious fanatic is trying to post them in a public place, you don't hear much about them. The irony is that even most folks who would sign a petition in favor of keeping them painted on a courtroom wall probably couldn't recite them. Can you? Don't feel bad—you're not alone. A United Press International survey from a few years ago revealed that only 68 of 200 Anglican priests polled could name all Ten Commandments, but half said they believed in space aliens.[1]

So don't kick yourself if all ten don't come to mind instantly. Instead, be proactive. Open your Bible to Exodus 20 and do your own personal review. If it's been a while, you may be quite surprised to see that

God's laws still apply today. More than that, following them opens the door to a life of great purpose and fulfillment for you and your family. Indeed, they may even be the secret to life.

Checking the List

The Ten Commandments work. Human experience over the last three and a half millennia proves it. Even if they don't agree on the source, the world's greatest thinkers validate the principles. And common sense confirms them. Ten fairly clear rules. Understand them and embrace them, and this whole silly world might suddenly make more sense.

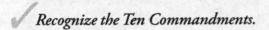 *Recognize the Ten Commandments.*

Go to Funerals

Every few years there's a news story about some guy who specified in his will that his last wish was to be buried in his car. The evening newscast treats us to a video of a 1973 Pontiac or 1941 Studebaker being lowered into an extra-wide grave. It's reminiscent of the Egyptian pharaohs, who were typically entombed with all kinds of gear and provisions for their upcoming journey into the afterlife. On occasion, even a few mistresses, servants, and pets were tossed in so the mummy wouldn't be lonely along the way.

These stories are news because they don't happen very often. Most funerals aren't about the dearly departed's possessions. Instead, the memories, conversation, tributes, and photo albums more often focus on relationships.

When a son or daughter delivers a eulogy, they don't talk about money spent on things; they talk about time spent together. Business associates may mention how "Dan was a fierce negotiator," or "Lenya was a tech wizard," but the reflections that mean the most will be about moments of kindness, generosity, availability, and courage.

Photographs on display are typically filled with people, not possessions. If a younger version of the deceased happens to be posed in front of a shiny Ford or classic VW, you can be sure there's a story to go along with it. If they're posing with a trophy, blue ribbon, craft project, or string of walleye pike, you know the photo is not really about what they're holding. The photographer is capturing a moment as friends and fans celebrate an experience.

Memorial services reveal that a person's character is more treasured than their cash value. If you attend a funeral where that is not the case, the atmosphere is tainted with awkward silences, inconsequential small talk, and forced accolades. I wouldn't want to be lying in that casket.

Put another way, there are funerals that leave you blessed and funerals that leave you pained. No funeral is fun. And there's great agony anytime the service is for a younger man, woman, or child whose life seemed to be cut short. But if you attend a memorial service with an attitude of respect and receptivity, there's much to gain. You'll see that personal glory is much too small a thing to live for. Honor comes in living and dying for something much bigger than ourselves.

The ancient Greek philosopher Epicurus was on to something when he said, "The art of living well and the art of dying well are one."

If a person's legacy is measured solely by the size of their estate, conversations after their death will focus on how their fortune is distributed between heirs who happen to be suffering little remorse. How sad is that?

The argument can be made that such a person wasted both their life and death. Matthew 16:26 (NASB) confirms, "For what will it profit a man if he gains the whole world and forfeits his soul?"

Attending funerals should be on the bucket list of every thoughtful individual. Not as some kind of morbid hobby, but as a reminder of the value of life and the inevitability of death.

If I still had my '66 VW, I might consider trying to take it with me into the afterlife. I think it would do well on those heavenly streets paved with gold. Unfortunately, it got scrapped back in 1975 after I rolled it on an icy entrance ramp to the Eisenhower expressway. My cars since then have been a long procession of nondescript hatchbacks and minivans.

My funeral may not make the evening news. But in a very real sense, I'm looking forward to it. Hope you can make it.

Checking the List

Live for something you can't hold on to, and you'll never fear death. As Jesus said in John 12:25, "Anyone who loves their life will lose it, while anyone who hates their life in this world will keep it for eternal life."

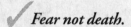 *Fear not death.*

Love and Be Loved

Newborns need to be held. They need to be cuddled and swaddled. They need to feel the warmth of skin on skin and the rhythm of Mom's or Dad's heartbeat. Think about where they just came from!

Pediatricians confirm newborns actually require a significant amount of physical contact every day. If they don't get it, they suffer from a withdrawal condition known as failure to thrive. Also called maternal deprivation syndrome, it's a psychosocial condition common in understaffed orphanages around the world, and it can be fatal. The health guide from the *New York Times* explains the causes, symptoms, treatment, and outlook.

Causes

> The majority of cases of failure to thrive in infants and young children (under two years old) are not caused by disease. Most cases are caused by dysfunctional caregiver interaction, poverty, child abuse, and parental ignorance about appropriate child care. Such cases are considered "nonorganic" failure to thrive...

Symptoms

- decreased or absent linear growth
- lack of appropriate hygiene
- interaction problems between mother and child
- weight less than the fifth percentile…

Treatment

Treatment of failure to thrive is a major undertaking which requires the input of a multidisciplinary team including physicians, nutritionists, social workers, behavioral specialists, and visiting nurses…

Outlook

With adequate attention and care, full recovery is expected. However, neglect severe enough to cause failure to thrive can kill if it continues.[2]

Years ago, traveling as a radio producer for the Josh McDowell Ministry, I had the rare privilege of visiting several orphanages in Russia and will never forget watching a single nurse care for a ward full of infants. With so little human contact, it's hard to imagine those babies growing into healthy adults who reach their God-given potential.

Without appearing heartless, I'm hoping to spin a positive lesson here. If diminished interaction leads to a failure to thrive, then conversely, extensive physical contact helps babies develop into kids who grow tall and strong, interact lovingly with others, and reach their full potential.

I can tell you firsthand that love is a powerful force. Over a period of several years, my wife, Rita, and I have welcomed ten foster babies into our home. Mostly newborn. Some had been exposed to cocaine in their mother's womb, which meant these babies were essentially recovering addicts. I will never forget our son Max holding one of those precious newborns while she was experiencing severe withdrawal tremors. This was when Max was an all-conference fullback, a state-qualifying wrestler, and starting catcher for a baseball team that placed fourth in state. He was a tough kid with a high threshold for pain. But watching that baby shake uncontrollably because of a birth mother's selfish choices broke Max's heart and made him a little angry. After the tremors subsided, he gently handed the tiny girl to Rita and then growled, "How could a mother do this to her baby?"

The good news is that "love never fails" (1 Corinthians 13:8). My wife and kids quite literally loved the residual cocaine right out of those babies. The boys and girls we've been able to keep track of over the years are doing very, very well.

All of which points to the desperate need we all have to receive love. And also to give love. When you snuggle, kiss, and sway with a newborn, love is flowing both directions. When a friend listens and talks you through a personal crisis, you are receiving and giving love. When a daughter visits the Alzheimer's unit in a nursing home to spend time with her mother who doesn't even remember who she is, that's still two-way love.

Pure, unselfish, mutual love is proof of a relationship with Christ. John 13:35 says, "By this everyone will know that you are my disciples, if you love one another."

The single best example of love flowing two directions is between man and his Creator. In 1 John 4:19, the Bible identifies the only reason we can love at all: "We love because he first loved us." Everything that comes from God flows out of his love for us. And the only reason we can offer authentic love to anyone is that God gave us that ability.

Knowing how to love and freely accepting love are among the most important items you will find on God's bucket list for any of us. If you didn't learn that in your first year of life, then spend some time right now considering how much you have to give and how worthy you are to receive.

Which brings up a major stumbling block so many people have

with God. They think, "How could God love someone like me?" "I'm not worthy." "My own daddy didn't love me, so I'm sure God doesn't."

The answer to those concerns is surprisingly simple. How can God love you? Because that's what he does. It's who he is. God is love. He knows everything about you. He knows your fears and your dreams. He knows your past, present, and future. He knows your achievements and failures. And yet he still loves you unconditionally. He has a wonderful plan for your life and has given you specific gifts, experiences, and abilities to make that plan come true.

He loved you so much that he created you. And he loves you so much that even though you've chosen many times to turn your back on him, he still sent his Son to pay the price for that sin by allowing Jesus to be nailed on a cross as your substitute. Then three days later, Jesus was resurrected from the dead to claim victory over death and open the gates of heaven to you. Most amazing of all, he loves you so much that he would have done all that even if you were the only person on earth!

Checking the List

Love is the greatest paradox of all. The term is used to describe how we feel about cars, candy bars, pizza, celebrities, and pets. We use the word selfishly when we shouldn't. And we don't use it during situations when we really should speak it loud and clear.

The word is more than a word. It's more than a feeling. As a noun, it's a gift. As a verb, it's a responsibility.

Love may very well be the ultimate test we all need to pass. First John 4:7-8 says, "Everyone who loves has been born of God and knows God. Whoever does not love does not know God, because God is love."

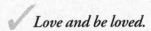 *Love and be loved.*

Don't Put God in a Box

As lovely as that last chapter was, here's a warning. Don't put God in a box labeled with the single word "Love." Yes, God is love. But that truth is often tragically misinterpreted.

A well-meaning person might say, wear, post, or display those three words—"God is love"—without even realizing the damage being done. Our human limitations prevent us from accurately defining what love is or who God is. Reducing God to a single concept—even the wonderful idea of love—is dangerous territory.

God is love…and more. God is truth. God is justice. God is life. God is mercy. God is righteousness. God is sovereign.

Millions of people on the planet are looking for love in their lives. Many have been looking in the wrong places and making devastating choices. Which means they're hurting. They need God to be mercy and truth.

Millions more have suffered tragedies that make them question why God allows bad things to happen to good people. They need God to be alive and sovereign.

Millions more have dedicated themselves to loving and serving but have still been broken by the inhumanity and darkness of this fallen world. They need God to be justice and righteousness.

The truth is, we all need God to be all those things. The Bible has been accurately described as God's love letter to each one of us. That idea is still not big enough to capture all of God's glory. He is beyond our imagination. The controversial theologian David Jenkins, bishop of Durham, put it this way: "No statement about God is simply, literally true. God is far more than can be measured, described, defined in ordinary language, or pinned down to any particular happening."

Do you know someone in need? Don't hand them God in a box. That's way too small.

If they're hurting, your best response is to come alongside and let them see God's compassion reflected in your life. Start with empathy, hope, and gentleness. Let them know "weeping may last through the night, but joy comes with the morning" (Psalm 30:5 NLT).

If they're living without purpose, remind them that they are loved and God is faithful. Let them know God's promise in Jeremiah 29:11—"'For I know the plans I have for you,' declares the LORD, 'plans to prosper you and not to harm you, plans to give you hope and a future.'"

If they're antagonistic toward God, make sure you tell your own story of how you were lost and found. Remember what Jesus told the formerly demon-possessed man in Mark 5:19: "Go home to your own people and tell them how much the Lord has done for you."

We are God's ambassadors every time we show compassion, help a friend see hope for the future, or share our own personal story. Those are all things we can do right in the moment. Later, the role expands when we are intentional about introducing people to the all-powerful, all-knowing, and all-present God of the universe. That will probably require words. Clear words that explain as best we can how God doesn't fit in a box. We can know him. We can even communicate with him. But we cannot comprehend his majesty.

Finally, here's an even better idea than coming alongside those who are hurting, frustrated, or doubting. Reach them *before* they hit bottom. Introduce them to the Creator of the universe early, and the Spirit of God will help them see how every aspect of their lives fits into the larger plan. Trouble may still come, but they'll see the bigger picture and trust that somehow the pieces all fit.

Finally, this should go without saying. Please let's not be so foolish that we try to stuff God in a box we keep in a closet and pull out only on Christmas, Easter, and the occasional wedding and funeral.

Checking the List

It's actually kind of silly when mere humans attempt to define God. We should acknowledge that God can never really be described in words, captured on chapel ceilings, chipped out of stone, or identified in hymns. But you can't blame us for trying. After all, he is the Alpha and the Omega of all we see, hear, and touch. And our entire lives should revolve around his relationship with us.

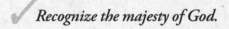 *Recognize the majesty of God.*

Come to the Garden

For more than two decades, I've been privileged to work with some amazing ministries doing amazing work.

As a freelance radio producer, I've helped raise funds to send Bibles to every corner of the world for the Bible League International, support pastors in Russia for the Josh McDowell Ministry, build homes in Kentucky for the Christian Appalachian Project, deliver Christmas gifts to the children of inmates for Prison Fellowship, rescue young women from human trafficking for Stella's Voice, sponsor screenings of *The Jesus Film* in African villages, distribute buckets of food and supplies to Malawi for Feed the Hungry, meet the needs of the homeless through CityTeam Rescue Missions, and support the wide range of services of the Salvation Army.

I continue to be blessed by the integrity of these organizations and the work they do. Helping real people with real needs. Many of the personal stories I have recorded and shared over the airways have blown me away. One stands out.

Years ago, while working with the Bible League International, I got hold of a scratchy, echoey recording of a pastor in China who had been arrested and tortured and spent much of his imprisonment at the bottom of a 15-foot pit filled with human waste. On the tape, the veteran pastor had recorded part of a song he sang while wading in that cesspool.

When I first heard the recording, I immediately sensed a reality to his joyfulness that was difficult to believe. You could hear the delight in his voice as he sang the old hymn "In the Garden." The song was written by C. Austin Miles in 1912. It wasn't in the hymnbook of the church I attended growing up, but I was vaguely familiar with it. The hymn has been recorded by Doris Day, Elvis Presley, Johnny Cash, and Willie Nelson. Hollywood has used it in several films, including *Nashville* and *Places in the Heart*. The tune is haunting, the lyrics simple and heartfelt.

> I come to the garden alone
> while the dew is still on the roses
> and the voice I hear falling on my ear
> the Son of God discloses.
>
> And he walks with me, and he talks with me,
> and he tells me I am his own;
> and the joy we share as we tarry there,
> none other has ever known.
>
> He speaks, and the sound of his voice,
> is so sweet the birds hush their singing,
> and the melody that he gave to me
> within my heart is ringing.
>
> I'd stay in the garden with him
> though the night around me be falling,
> but he bids me go; thru the voice of woe
> his voice to me is calling.

Through a translator, the old pastor explained that when he was in the cesspool, the guards would leave him alone. There was no torture or outside disturbances. The once disgusting pit had become his private worship space. His garden.

That Chinese pastor is a living, breathing example of Psalm 5:11—"Let all who take refuge in you be glad; let them ever sing for joy."

I think of that pastor often. And it may sound irrational, but I'm a little jealous. Really. Maybe if you heard that recording, you'd believe me. To experience true joy regardless of your comfort, situation, or status must be deeply satisfying.

I can't cross that concept off my bucket list quite yet, but I'm working on it. I invite you to do the same.

Checking the List

You don't need many of them, but I pray you'll experience a handful of breakthrough spiritual moments that penetrate your heart, mind, and soul all at the same time. Those are truths worth hanging on to. You can come back to them again and again. I'm afraid those insights typically don't come without laying a little groundwork. You need to open a devotional, sit in a pew, dust off your Bible, or tune in to Christian radio. It might also help if you sit regularly with a small group of friends, listening to their stories. And maybe sharing some of your own.

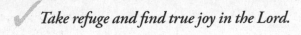 *Take refuge and find true joy in the Lord.*

Put a Price on Your Head

M any people think too highly of themselves.

They believe the world owes them big-time. They walk around feeling surrounded by constant praise. Why does that happen to some and not others? Perhaps it was because they had it too easy growing up. Mom (or a maid) picked up their clothes. Dad never said no. Maybe they are just so beautiful and so clever that the world around them simply falls at their feet. Maybe it just happens.

If good things come a little too easy to you, you could probably use a dose of humility and appreciation for what you have. One recommendation might be to intentionally leave your comfort zone. Consider taking up a challenging hobby that forces you to ask others for help. Make a mission trip to a third-world nation. Or make an anonymous sacrificial gift to a worthy charity, telling no one. Embrace the passage of Scripture that says, "From everyone who has been given much, much will be demanded" (Luke 12:48). That realization and those kinds of activities might be exactly what you need to fully understand your place in this world.

On the other hand, just as many people don't understand how wonderful they are.

They live a pained existence that doesn't seem to have much purpose. They walk around feeling surrounded by constant scorn. Why does that happen to some and not others? Perhaps they experienced physical or emotional abuse as a child. Mom didn't hold them. Dad was too busy or too brutal. Never a kind word was said. Maybe they are just so filled with fear, depression, and anxiety that they see no hope for the future. Maybe it just happens.

If not-so-good things continue to crush your spirit and leave you feeling broken and burdened, you could probably use a healthy dose of encouragement and a refresher course in identifying your many undiscovered gifts. One recommendation might be to intentionally engage in activities that allow you to shine and feel appreciated. Consider taking up a challenging hobby that forces you to develop a new skill. Make a mission trip to a third-world nation. Or make an anonymous sacrificial gift to a worthy charity, telling no one. Embrace the passage of Scripture that says, "The LORD is close to the brokenhearted and saves those who are crushed in spirit" (Psalm 34:18). That realization and those kinds of activities might be exactly what you need to fully understand your place in this world.

Of course, we all need both. We need to experience humility and empowerment. We need to see life as a gift and a challenge. We need to feel beautiful and useful. We need to feel worthy and wanted. Those needs are universal, not limited by economic status, IQ, athleticism, race, gender, or religious background.

The pivotal idea to jot down on your bucket list is to remember that all human life has value. This chapter is not about suicide prevention, but it could be. This is not an antiabortion message, but it could be that too. This is about encouraging each of us as individuals to answer the question, "What is the value of my life?" Scientists tell us we are 60 percent water, and I ran across a website claiming that the rest of the elements in our physical bodies are worth about $160. I hope we aren't judged on our chemical makeup.

The true value of something is not really about cash. The money in your wallet is just ink on paper. Value is determined by identifying something for which it can be exchanged. For example, a cup of fancy coffee at Starbucks costs about what you'd pay for a new baseball. The cost of a sunroom addition is about what you'd pay for a Lexus or for a single year at an Ivy League school.

So what is the value of your life? Someone has already demonstrated the exact value of your life by trading his life for yours. That's right, you are worth Jesus. Theologians sometimes even call Jesus's substitutionary death "the great exchange." As a matter of fact, Jesus loves you so much that even if you were the only person who ever lived, he would have died on the cross to pay the penalty for your sins.

One of the most accurate descriptions of Jesus is Servant King. He died to serve. He lives to reign. As the ultimate role model, Jesus also has the answer to both of the human conditions described above.

Those who are thinking a little too highly of themselves need to be reminded that at the Last Supper, Jesus took a basin of water and washed the feet of the disciples. You would also do well to read this reminder from the Gospels:

> Whoever wants to become great among you must be your servant, and whoever wants to be first must be your slave— just as the Son of Man did not come to be served, but to serve, and to give his life as a ransom for many (Matthew 20:26-28).

Those who are thinking too poorly of themselves need to be reminded they can be heirs to God's kingdom. Not because of anything they can do, but because of what Jesus's love and mercy has already done.

> He saved us, not because of righteous things we had done, but because of his mercy. He saved us through the washing of rebirth and renewal by the Holy Spirit, whom he poured out on us generously through Jesus Christ our Savior, so that, having been justified by his grace, we might become heirs having the hope of eternal life (Titus 3:5-7).

Checking the List

Because we're human, we deny our sinful condition. "Hey, at least I'm not as bad as that guy." At the same time, we can't even conceive of how much God loves us. "How could the Creator of the universe care about me?" We forget that when we put our faith and trust in Jesus, the infinite price of our sins has been paid by the infinite love of God.[3]

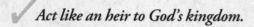 *Act like an heir to God's kingdom.*

Get Fired

During college, I spent two summers as a waiter. One stint in a family burger pub and the other in a white-tablecloth restaurant that catered to little old ladies.

I think everyone should work in the restaurant business for at least one summer. Waiting tables or flipping burgers will give you a great appreciation for anyone who works in food service. You'll be a better guest and a better tipper.

Everyone should also spend some time in commission sales. It will teach you to hustle and appreciate the value of a paycheck.

And I also think everyone should get fired at least once. That's one of those involuntary bucket-list items with benefits. You'll know what it's like to hit bottom.

Out of college, my first full-time job was selling photocopiers for the A.B. Dick Company. Not Xerox. Not Canon. Not IBM. A.B. Dick. The employee turnover rate resembled a revolving door. I lasted two years.

My second full-time job was selling law books to corporate attorneys. I was terrible at it. For almost two years I lugged a 28-pound briefcase around Chicago's loop, changing career paths just weeks before I was due to be terminated for repeatedly missing my sales quota.

My third job was as a novice copywriter for a tiny ad agency on Chicago's famed Michigan Avenue. They hired me after landing the assignment to name and brand Frito Lay's SunChips. When that project finished they could no longer afford my minuscule salary. I was let go on my wife's twenty-sixth birthday.

My fourth job was as a copywriter for a much larger agency with accounts like Midway Airlines, Kroger, and Corona Beer. Over five years, I produced a ton of sparkling work and even wrote some jingles. A new hotshot creative director came in and cleaned house, firing me on my thirty-first birthday, two days after my fourth child was born. I begged for another chance, and they let me hang around another six months.

My fifth job was at Domain Communications, a small agency and recording studio in the suburbs that served Christian ministries and publishers. The fit was perfect, but one year later we merged with two other small agencies and the creative department moved to Seattle, leaving me once again without a full-time job.

My sixth job was not a job at all. For more than 20 years, I have been a freelance writer, producer, author, creativity trainer, speaker, and consultant. As you can imagine, technology and social media have forced me to grow in ways I never imagined. But that's not all bad. And I've threatened to fire myself only a dozen times or so.

Looking back, I see God's hand in every one of those devastating job losses and career changes. During those times, if someone would have quoted the Bible verse that says, "In all things God works for the good of those who love him, who have been called according to his purpose" (Romans 8:28), I may have strangled them. But now I see that it really is true. I can connect the dots from who I was to who I am. It's crystal clear that I am using skills developed in the midst of adversity to do things I would never have dreamed possible. God really does work all things for the good.

Checking the List

God uses it all. The good stuff and the bad. Search your heart, and you may realize that while victories are nice, you learned more and grew closer to God during your most painful losses. Trophies just sit on a shelf or gather dust. Scars stay with you and prove you're a survivor.

 Treasure your opportunities to be an overcomer.

No Excuses

The way-too-friendly guy down the street is taller, has whiter teeth, and makes more money than you. That annoying woman in your book club has better taste, better hair, and better kids than you. Face it, my friend, you are less than perfect.

Well, join the club. I have terrible knees, tinnitus, a retreating hairline, and the inability to remember names of people I just met. While we're at it, let's admit that just about every one of us had acne in high school and made one or two poor decisions in our late teens.

Phew. Considering all these flaws, I think it's pretty clear that God cannot possibly use any of us. As a matter of fact, I'm officially starting a club for people too broken to be of any use to God.

Hmm…who else could we recruit for our club? Check out this group of 25 individuals worthy of becoming charter members. This list has been kicking around the Internet for a while. You can find it on blogs, websites, and even a poster by Slingshot Publishing. The list is an eye-opening reminder that God uses broken people to do great things.

> Noah was a drunk.
> Abraham was too old.
> Isaac was a daydreamer.
> Jacob was a liar.

Leah was ugly.

Joseph was abused.

Moses had a stuttering problem.

Gideon was afraid.

Samson had long hair and was a womanizer.

Rahab was a harlot.

David had an affair and was a murderer.

Elijah was suicidal.

Isaiah preached naked.

Jeremiah and Timothy were too young.

Jonah ran from God.

Naomi was a widow.

Job went bankrupt.

Martha worried about everything.

The Samaritan woman was divorced.

Zacchaeus was too small.

Lazarus was dead.

The disciples fell asleep while praying.

Peter denied Christ.

Paul was too religious.

Timothy had an ulcer.

The weaknesses listed are true, but biblical scholars would certainly balk at labeling these historical characters so simplistically. There's a story of sweet victory behind each one of them. For example, Noah was the only man in his generation who followed God, but in his later years he endured a drunken stupor. That failing reminds us how not even a flood could wipe away the wickedness of the world.

Jacob deceived his father and stole the birthright from his older brother, but he would become the father of the 12 tribes of Israel. The Bible doesn't exactly say Leah was ugly, but it does say her little sister was prettier. Still, through Leah's son Judah, God would trace the lineage of Jesus. Rahab was a prostitute, but she courageously hid advance scouts for the Israelites, helping them win the battle for Jericho.

In the New Testament, the Samaritan woman at the well had multiple husbands but gave testimony of Jesus to her entire town. Outside the Garden of Gethsemane, the disciples fell asleep when they were supposed to be praying, but later they boldly spread the gospel. Before his conversion, Paul held the cloaks of the men who stoned Stephen, the very first Christian martyr. The experience became part of Paul's testimony of God's grace (Acts 22:20).

Are you feeling too old, too short, or too broke? Consider Abraham, Zacchaeus, and Job. Are you a worrywart, like Martha? Or running from God, like Jonah? Do you have a speech impediment, like Moses? Do you have tummy troubles, like Timothy? Maybe you've been labeled a long-haired upstart, like Samson.

Ladies and gentlemen, there is still a place for you in God's great story. Not because you're perfect, but because you have been called. Chosen by God.

> Brothers and sisters, think of what you were when you were called. Not many of you were wise by human standards; not many were influential; not many were of noble birth. But God chose the foolish things of the world to shame the wise; God chose the weak things of the world to shame the strong. God chose the lowly things of this world and the despised things—and the things that are not—to nullify the things that are, so that no one may boast before him (1 Corinthians 1:26-29).

From addictions to shyness. From sibling rivalry to abuse. God can use you just as you are. That's the foundational message of the gospel. There is a plan for each and every one of us. Whether we are broken by sin or simply experiencing a difficult season, we are all in need of a Savior. His love. His example. His grace.

A reminder to review this list of 25 imperfect people mightily used by God belongs on your bucket list. There are several ways the list may come in handy.

You could search your Bible for the complete stories of these historical characters and do your own month-long Bible study.

When you meet someone feeling downcast because they exhibit one of these characteristics—a widow, a sex addict, an alcoholic, a stutterer—don't judge, and don't dismiss their fears and discouragement. Instead, point them to a biblical narrative with which they can identify.

Finally, keep this page bookmarked as a reminder of how God welcomes broken people into his family. God often empowers individuals to be examples of how he gives healing, strength, wisdom, new purpose, and hero status. Some he even raises from the dead.

Checking the List

What's your favorite go-to excuse?

"I'm too busy." "Other people are much more qualified." "I have nothing to wear." "I tried that once, and it didn't go well." "I have a bad back." "I don't like the person in charge." "I'm not a people person." "It's too cold." "It's too hot." "That's too far." "They never listen to my ideas." "I've never done that before."

Did you just read your favorite excuse? Circle it! If your favorite wasn't included, write it down at the bottom of this page. You certainly don't want to forget it, right? Because if you forget your excuse, you won't have it anymore.

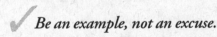 *Be an example, not an excuse.*

Bounce Off Brick Walls

The stickball diamond behind Fox Ridge School was a home plate drawn with chalk, a sewer grate for first, the corner of the four-square grid for second, and the basketball stanchion as third. A rectangle of athletic tape on the brick wall of the gymnasium served as the strike zone. That wall was less than two feet from home plate.

There's no sliding in blacktop stickball, but of course you can always overrun home. Which I did. And when I put my hands out to slow myself, I miscalculated the distance between home and brick and felt something snap in my right wrist.

I played another inning or two, finally telling my sons and the neighborhood boys that I was calling it quits for the day. They called me mean names, which was totally acceptable because I may have politely trash talked them a bit earlier in the game.

I favored the right wrist for several days before seeing Dr. Showalter, the best hand surgeon in town. He confirmed the carpal lunate bone in my right wrist was broken. We scheduled surgery for the right wrist, and just to make sure, a surgical prep nurse actually drew an X on my right wrist.

I recall it was my right wrist for three reasons. There's still a small scar. Twenty years later it still tweaks a bit. And before surgery about a zillion additional members of the hospital staff asked me which wrist they were cutting into.

Maybe it wasn't quite a zillion, but clearly no one wanted to cut into the wrong wrist. And that's a good thing. When surgeons are about to slice through your skin, you want their hands to proceed with confidence. You want them well trained. You want them well rested. You want them working in sync with the rest of the surgical team. And you want them to cut into the right body part.

You don't want to spend any more time under anesthesia than necessary, but you do want them to be smart, take their time, and get it right. As Proverbs 19:2 (NLT) tells us, "Enthusiasm without knowledge is no good; haste makes mistakes."

It's all part of a larger life strategy and lesson for your bucket list that says, "Don't make bad things worse." Examples? When you drop your wallet in the fish tank, remove your wristwatch before fishing it out. After you walk through a yard filled with dog poop, make sure you check your shoes before walking on the carpet. When you're lost, stop and ask directions before driving 20 miles the wrong way. When a cop pulls you over for a minor traffic violation, don't call him nasty names.

And if you work on a surgical team, check multiple times before making that first incision. You'll save everyone involved pain, suffering, frustration, and a possible lawsuit.

As it turns out, stuff happens.

Right in the middle of a nice friendly game of stickball, some knucklehead runs into a brick wall and breaks a bone. It doesn't help to point fingers of blame. That brick wall is not at fault. The designer of the ball diamond is not at fault. Even the base runner is not really at fault. After all, it was an accident. But it does help to assess the situation and make an informed and reasonable decision on how to proceed. Lawyers call that due diligence.

Refusing to go to a doctor or cutting into the wrong limb are the kind of decisions that take the situation from bad to worse. Minor setbacks are part of life. Piling on guilt, regret, blame, shame, and second-guessing adds a load of heavy-handed baggage no one should carry.

Checking the List

You're going to run into an occasional brick wall. When that happens, you have several options.

You can ignore the problem. Which means any damage will not be rectified. Plus, there's a good chance you'll run into the same wall again on a later occasion.

You can lay in a crumpled heap on the ground feeling sorry for yourself. Which means someone else has to come to your rescue and nurse you back to health.

You can go way overboard with your reaction—tearing down the wall, making stickball illegal, and throwing out all your sneakers so you are never tempted to run again.

Or you can bounce off the brick wall. Which means absorbing the hit, assessing the damage, seeking out a professional opinion, and making sure you don't make a bad situation worse.

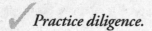 *Practice diligence.*

Redefine Vacation

Are family vacations on God's bucket list?

I'm recalling the infamous Payleitner family trek to our nation's capital. One dad, one mom, five kids. One minivan. The road trip takes us from Chicago to Washington, DC, and back. Our oldest, Alec, is heading into his senior year of high school. Rae Anne is four. The three middle children—Randy, Max and Isaac—endure constantly changing levels of mutual love, laughter, and pounding.

The budget and schedule are both tight. Early one morning, I leave our cramped DC hotel room and drive to the Federal Triangle. The plan is for me to acquire time-stamped tickets to the White House for later that day and swing back and pick up my relaxed and well-rested family. The timing is perfect, except for one small hitch. The White House is closed for public tours that day.

I overcome my frustration by jogging three blocks and securing a coveted position third in line for the tour of the FBI building, which features lots of guns and secret-agent stuff. Not a bad second choice. The doors are scheduled to open in 45 minutes, which I figure is plenty of time for Rita to get the crew up, dressed, and through the easy-to-navigate Metro. As scores of tourists begin to line up behind me, I call Rita with very specific instructions about where, when, and how to get to my location outside the FBI gates. Piece of cake, right?

I wasn't there, but Rita tells a slightly different story. Alec heroically gets his brothers ready to go. My wife wrestles our young and feisty daughter into a cute little outfit. Hand in hand, the six of them hustle over to, down in, on, off, and up from the Metro. A couple blocks from the FBI building, sweet Rae Anne stops in her tracks, yanks her hands out from the grasp of her mom and oldest brother, and fiercely asks the obvious question, "What's a vacation again?"

At the time it wasn't funny. But as you may imagine, the story has taken on a life of its own. Even now, when a family member schedules too many activities during a long weekend, they'll stop in their tracks and do their best impression of four-year-old Rae Anne: "What's a vacation again?"

The story actually doesn't end there. At about the time my family is zooming through subterranean DC, the tour guides at the FBI decide to open the gates early, and literally hundreds of tourists funnel past me, queuing up for their turn inside. My cherished third place in line is a moot point by the time my family reaches my side. Our tour finally begins some two hours later. Like I said, it wasn't funny at the time. I guess you had to be there.

But probably you *have* been there. Vacations that leave you exhausted. Picnics with ants. Camping with leaky tents. Beach trips with sunburns and sandy sandwiches. Excursions to the city complete with dark alleys and lost cabbies. The fishing trip with nothing biting but the mosquitoes.

It makes you wonder whether family vacations are worth the trouble. More significantly, whether such a huge investment of time, money, and emotions is important to God. The Bible doesn't say a lot about vacations. The traveling described in the Bible was usually out of necessity and typically not very pleasant. Noah's unlikely cruise. The Israelites' 40-year trek through the desert. Abraham didn't need to leave home; his in-tents life seemed to be one relocation after another. Paul's well-documented journeys were not vacations at all, but mission trips. The purpose of Joseph and Mary's road trip to Bethlehem was clearly not relaxation; it was to fulfill the census requirement and unknowingly fulfill prophecy. Besides, soon-to-be-dad Joseph failed to make hotel reservations.

But God did endorse rest and even insist on it. God himself rested on the seventh day of creation. He established the Sabbath as a day of rest in the Ten Commandments. Right in the middle of one of the busiest and most emotional times of their ministry, Jesus instructed the apostles to take a break.

> The apostles gathered around Jesus and reported to him all they had done and taught. Then, because so many people were coming and going that they did not even have a chance to eat, he said to them, "Come with me by yourselves to a quiet place and get some rest." So they went away by themselves in a boat to a solitary place (Mark 6:30-32).

When it comes to nurturing a healthy family, the first two verses of Psalm 127 help put your priorities in order.

> Unless the LORD builds a house, the work of the builders is wasted…It is useless for you to work so hard from early morning until late at night, anxiously working for food to eat; for God gives rest to his loved ones (NLT).

The message is clear. God is more important than work. He is the true architect and builder of your home and life. There's no way that work alone—even long hours of toil and sweat—can provide for your family. Workaholics need to trust God at work and at rest.

So whether you do Disney, check into a bed-and-breakfast, stroll a beach, gape at Manhattan skyscrapers, or simply hibernate at home, don't forget to take an occasional vacation. For some people, rest is doing nothing. For others, rest is doing anything other than work. For families especially, rest is setting aside time to make memories.

Time apart from the daily grind gives us opportunity to reflect on our purpose and our story. That's what sets us apart from the world. In other words, that's what makes us holy.

Is visiting the top of the Empire State Building or snorkeling the Great Barrier Reef on your bucket list? Go for it. As for me and my house, our vacation goals have always been simply to make memories that bring a smile and to gather a story I can tell. Mission accomplished.

Checking the List

When you tell your story, make sure to honor and include both work and play. Especially the stories that have become family legend. I wouldn't trade the memory of those three days in our nation's capital for anything. If you had asked me in the middle of it, I might have had a different answer.

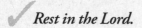 *Rest in the Lord.*

Entertain Angels

You don't have to believe all the stories you hear of angels. But you should believe some of them. Angels are real. And you can expect that during the course of your life, you're going to come across an angel or two and not even know it.

One grown woman vividly recalls the day her mom dropped her off at school back in sixth grade. They were running late and had parked across the street from their normal drop-off zone. The distracted girl began to step into traffic but was lifted off the ground and pulled back to the car. A pickup truck whooshed by inches in front of her, but the woman remembers feeling as if the event happened in slow motion. When she turned breathlessly to thank her mother for pulling her to safety, the girl realized her mother had watched the entire scene unfold from much too far away to have reached her in time. The heroic hand that saved her life was not from this world. The scene sounds like something described in Psalm 91:11-12—"He will command his angels concerning you to guard you in all your ways; they will lift you up in their hands."

A mother and father nod to the hospital chaplain joining them in silent prayer at the bedside of their son, who's barely clinging to life. They expect the chaplain to offer a few obligatory prayers and move to the next room. Instead, still without speaking, the older gentleman sits with the couple in vigil for the entire night. When the sun comes up, a flurry of doctors and nurses hustle in and out of the room as the boy comes out of his coma. Only when things settle down do the parents attempt to find the chaplain who sat, prayed, and ushered a quiet strength into the room. The nurse in charge assures them that no chaplain was on duty that night. The entire family turns their life over to God, realizing they had been visited by an angel. Which is entirely possible. After all, Hebrews 1:14 says, "Are not all angels ministering spirits sent to serve those who will inherit salvation?"

Some of the stories of heroic angels, of course, can be explained in human terms. But there are enough stories around shared by thoughtful, even formerly skeptical individuals that you can be quite sure angels move in and out of our lives on a regular basis. The small child lost for days in a national park is protected and led to safety by "a nice man dressed in white." In a dark alley, thugs retreat from their assault because two massive dudes unexpectedly show up right behind the intended victim. A stranger pulls an accident victim out of a burning car but disappears before paramedics arrive.

Some church traditions may place a little too much emphasis on angels, but there is certainly precedent for all thinking Christians to honor and even expect angels to show up on God's command. After all, angels are referenced more than 200 times in the Bible.

In the Old Testament, God sent an army of angels with horses and chariots of fire to protect Elisha and his servant (2 Kings 6:8-23). Daniel describes how an angel shut the mouths of the lions he was facing (Daniel 6:22). In Acts 12, an angel helped Peter escape from prison. Paul faced a shipwreck with surprising calm because an angel had explained God's plan for the coming days (Acts 27:23-26).

It's also worth considering how often angels intervene and simply go undetected or unconfirmed. It's possible that your own life has been spared a dozen times because angels cleared a path or guided you down a safer route. Hebrews 13:2 (NLT) reminds us, "Don't forget to show hospitality to strangers, for some who have done this have entertained angels without realizing it!"

Angels, of course, are not just protectors and guardians. They encourage, lead worship, and deliver life-changing news. On separate occasions, angels appeared to Mary and Joseph, announcing the young couple's role as earthly parents to the Son of God. A multitude of the heavenly host appeared to the shepherds on the hills near Bethlehem and proclaimed, "Glory to God in the highest heaven, and on earth peace to those on whom his favor rests" (Luke 2:14). When three women visited Jesus's tomb on Easter morning and saw the stone had been rolled away, it was an angel who let them know what had really happened. "'Don't be alarmed,' he said. 'You are looking for Jesus the Nazarene, who was crucified. He has risen! He is not here'" (Mark 16:6).

So. Include believing in angels on your bucket list. Show them hospitality. At a time of need, feel free to ask God to send one your way—although you'll want to be vigilant because not all angels are the friendly kind. Some have been cast down into the darkness and serve Satan. These fallen angels are sometimes called demons, devils, or unclean spirits. Their existence is one more reason to entertain your own regiment of angels.

Checking the List

It's worth noting that you really shouldn't pray to your guardian angel, but certainly pray for God to send his angels to guide and protect you and all those friends and family members who mean so much to you.[4]

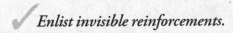 *Enlist invisible reinforcements.*

Shun Easy Money

Before picking up this book, did you already have your own bucket list? If so, I imagine it included something like "become a millionaire." That's a typical goal for many ambitious and talented people like you. And if you're close to reaching that goal, I applaud you. I trust you will save, invest, and be generous with your windfall. To help you manage your funds, I encourage you to dig into a Bible study on some of the 2300 Scripture verses on money and possessions. Here are just a few.

- "For the love of money is a root of all kinds of evil. Some people, eager for money, have wandered from the faith and pierced themselves with many griefs" (1 Timothy 6:10).

- "No one can serve two masters. Either you will hate the one and love the other, or you will be devoted to the one and despise the other. You cannot serve both God and money" (Matthew 6:24).

- "For where your treasure is, there your heart will be also" (Luke 12:34).

What do you love? Who is your master? Where is your treasure? All excellent questions. Especially in our culture, where money has a stranglehold on too many people.

If you're not even close to that goal of saving your first million, I need to warn you about a few things. First, don't sacrifice relationships in your pursuit. Money can't buy love or happiness. As a matter of fact, the Bible tells us the very pursuit of money breeds discontent. "Whoever loves money never has enough; whoever loves wealth is never satisfied with their income" (Ecclesiastes 5:10).

Second, please, please, please do not set your sights on easy money at places like Las Vegas, Atlantic City, or local gambling establishments, which seem to be popping up with more and more frequency these days. If the reputation of the people who run those establishments isn't enough to keep you away, consider how the number of new paupers walking out their glistening doors far outnumber big winners. Who do you think pays for the opulent architecture, electric bills, and high-tech security? Casinos stay in business by making money, not giving it away.

Third, even more disconcerting than casinos are state and national lotteries. They are run by the government, which should not be in the business of defrauding its citizens. Have you noticed that each time a lottery is due for a giant cash payout, a TV news reporter will visit some sleazy mini-mart, shove his or her microphone into the face of someone waiting in line to buy a ticket, and ask, "What would you do if you won the jackpot?"

I always feel a little angry toward the news reporter for hyping this con game. But most of the emotion that sweeps over me is a sadness for the folks in line.

These targeted victims are putting their hope in something that doesn't last. Even if they win, millions of dollars doesn't last into eternity. Why, it doesn't even last here on earth! It's easy to find stories of lottery winners who eventually declare bankruptcy. The National Endowment for Financial Education estimates that up to 70 percent of Americans who experience a sudden windfall lose that money within a few years.[5]

What's more, the tiny number of individuals who do win millions in the lottery are missing out on the satisfaction of earning their rewards the old-fashioned way—through hard work and savings.

If you still have your heart set on becoming a millionaire, stick to the proven formula. Earn an honest buck, pinch pennies, and invest prudently. Proverbs promises, "Wealth from get-rich-quick schemes quickly disappears; wealth from hard work grows over time" (Proverbs 13:11 NLT).

Checking the List

What's your definition of success? Is it stuff and more stuff? Or is it living to give glory to God? The lure and intoxication of wealth is a powerful temptation relentlessly drawing people away from God's real purpose for life and all the blessings that would follow.

The Bible teaches, "Those who want to get rich fall into temptation and a trap and into many foolish and harmful desires that plunge people into ruin and destruction" (1 Timothy 6:9). You've been warned.

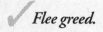 *Flee greed.*

Create

For a season of my working career—most of the 1980s and early '90s—I literally held the title of creative. At advertising agencies I worked for, new projects were launched at a meeting of a couple members of the account team, someone from Research, someone from Traffic, and a few creatives.

Looking back, I guess that single word was reasonable shorthand for art directors, copywriters, and creative directors. But you have to agree that it sounds a little self-indulgent and exclusionary. As if the act of being creative is limited only to elite individuals paid to design and write the ads.

I confess, I enjoyed the title. My younger self enjoyed the mystique and recognition when ideas from my very own imagination were transformed into spots, ads, point-of-purchase, and collateral for clients like Midway Airlines, Corona Beer, Kroger, Frito-Lay, and the Chicago Symphony Orchestra. Art directors and copywriters liked getting all the credit. We would never admit that we depended on clear direction and parameters from all the other departments. Sure, we were the creative department, but we couldn't really even begin our work until we received thoughtful positioning statements from the account team, constructive data from Research, and detailed specs and deadlines from Traffic. Today, I freely admit the work of all those departments requires creativity.

Of all the creatures on the earth, only humans can create. And *all* humans can create. We're made in the image of the Creator. Genesis 1:27 tells us, "So God created mankind in his own image, in the image of God he created them." Which is why humans alone have the unique gift of creativity.

As an aside, that's also why we are the only creatures who appreciate creativity. Do you think a shark appreciates the astonishing beauty of the fish swarming a coral reef? He's just grazing for dinner. Does a wildebeest appreciate the sunset on the African savannah? He's just biding his time as part of the food chain.

In 1998, two artists founded the Elephant Art and Conservation Project, which features and sells artwork painted by elephants. The most trainable of pachyderms will hold a brush in their trunk and thereby create abstract paintings. Humans place empty canvases in front of elephants that have been conditioned to create colorful and eye-pleasing designs, including self-portraits. It's an impressive feat. But please, let's not call it creativity or art.

So how should we humans use this gift? To do what God created us to do—give glory back to him. To shine a spotlight on all he is and all he does, as Jesus said in the Sermon on the Mount.

> You are the light of the world. A town built on a hill cannot be hidden. Neither do people light a lamp and put it under a bowl. Instead they put it on its stand, and it gives light to everyone in the house. In the same way, let your light shine before others, that they may see your good deeds and glorify your Father in heaven (Mathew 5:14-16).

Because you're human, let's assume being creative is on God's bucket list for you. How do you harness that gift?

It's not about doing whatever you want, wherever you want, however you want. That's not creativity. That's like turning loose a gaggle of two-year-olds with colored Sharpies in the White House. Such an undisciplined army would be only slightly more creative than elephants with paintbrushes.

Someone once said, "Necessity is the mother of invention." Put another way, if you want to be creative, find a need and fill it.

In Madison Avenue ad agencies, creative departments meet clients' need to deliver a message. For an advertising campaign, the other departments provide critical information, including the target audience, a unique selling proposition, budgets, and deadlines.

When Thomas Edison resolved to create a long-lasting incandescent lightbulb, he didn't just sit down one day in 1878 and say, "Maybe I'll invent something." He saw the need, assessed the available materials and technologies, and set the goal. More than 10,000 failures later, he famously had his "aha moment." That's why Edison really did say, "Genius is 1 percent inspiration, 99 percent perspiration."

Henry Ford saw the need to build cars more efficiently than one at a time on a factory floor. In 1913, he invented the moving assembly line, and Ford Motor Company began producing one car every 93 minutes.

Again, creativity is fundamental to every human endeavor, not just to inventing and advertising. It might be summarized this way: Whatever you're expected to do, do it well. Then, identify a gap or shortcoming in the process. Assess your resources. And persistently consider all the pieces of the puzzle until you have your very own aha moment.

For a farmer looking for a more efficient pattern for plowing, that could be using Google Maps to survey his fields. For an audiologist looking to increase her business, that might be focusing on aging disco dancers who listened to too much loud music in the 1970s. For FedEx, as they consider more efficient ways to delivery packages to remote locations, that might involve using drones.

For followers of Christ, the question of creativity has some urgency. We're not just seeking personal glory. We actually have a two-part task. Uncover how God wants us to invest our time, talent, and resources. And then do it with excellence and creativity. "For we are God's handiwork, created in Christ Jesus to do good works, which God prepared in advance for us to do" (Ephesians 2:10).

Checking the List

God took six days to create the earth. And it was perfect. His creative assignments for you might take a little longer than that. Initially you may not get it right. Which means persistence is probably the most critical element to creativity. So begin. And continue to ask God to plan your work—so you can work his plan for your life. As promised in the Bible, "I am certain that God, who began the good work within you, will continue his work until it is finally finished on the day when Christ Jesus returns" (Philippians 1:6 NLT).

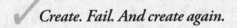 *Create. Fail. And create again.*

Get Schooled at the County Fair

Stroll a county fair recently? Did you ever stop by one of the carny booths to try your hand at a game of skill? I encourage you to give it your best shot, but don't count on winning. Instead, do it for the life lesson.

At the duck hunt, the rifle sights will be just a little bent. At the balloon-busting booth, the darts will be dull, and the balloons will be heavy-duty and underinflated, which makes them more difficult to pop. The basketball booth features rims that are oval, smaller than regulation, and higher than you expect. When you test your pitching arm, be aware that the bottles on the bottom of the milk-bottle pyramid are weighted and nearly impossible to knock over.

The lesson? Sometimes the easier it looks, the tougher it is.

Trying to impress a high school girlfriend, I was an easy target at the Kane County Fair in 1973. The carny lured Sally and me to his booth by "accidentally" dropping a certificate that promised one free game. After that first round, he quickly added up my score. That's when the act really began. He seemed genuinely distressed as he informed me that I was already 80 percent of the way toward winning my choice of the boom box or giant panda. Since I was just one good round away from victory, I played again. And again.

The con man quickly emptied my wallet. And just as quickly shooed the two of us away when he realized I was only good for 14 bucks. Most boys in that situation would stomp off cursing, but my curiosity kicked in. The carny had hustled me, and I was eager to decipher his methods.

Sally and I stood on the other side of the gravel midway, watching him scam several other unsuspecting teenagers. Adding up the possible points in my head, I realized the score from my initial "free game" was almost impossible to earn. He had given me lots of points, but there was no way I would do it again. Watching his methods, I actually began to appreciate his fast-talking pitch. I had never seen a hustler at work.

After watching three other guys open their wallets and pull out bill after bill, I didn't feel quite so bad. From 20 feet away it looked like I got off cheap. And the multiple lessons I learned that day for a mere 14 bucks have very likely served me well.

A few helpful verses from Scripture back up these lessons.

> If you think you are standing firm, be careful that you don't fall! (1 Corinthians 10:12).

We all need to be humbled. At 15, walking through the county fair with my girlfriend, I thought I was invincible. Most 15-year-old boys do. Oh, they have their inner doubts and insecurities. But until they're put in their place a few times by mentors, bosses, or con artists, they think they are smarter than everyone else. A dose of humility is not a bad thing. It reminds young men (and women) of their mortality and vulnerability.

> Watch out for false prophets. They come to you in sheep's clothing, but inwardly they are ferocious wolves (Matthew 7:15).

We all need to know that the world is full of deceivers and tempters, which means we need to guard our hearts and minds (and wallets). That carny was the friendliest guy in the world, tempting me with riches—a flashy boom box for me or a giant stuffed panda for Sally. And he kept up the charade until I was out of money. Don't feel bad for being tempted. Even Jesus was tempted. Just don't let yourself be deceived.

> As a dog returns to its vomit, so fools repeat their folly. Do you see a person wise in their own eyes? There is more hope for a fool than for them (Proverbs 26:11-12).

Finally, don't make the same mistake over and over again. Getting burned by a con artist when you're 15 can be a valuable experience—if you learn from it. Fools repeat their folly. They go back to the same carnival booth or blackjack table again and again, expecting a different outcome.

Maybe I should track down that carny—or the next one I see—and thank him for the lesson. I never got conned at a county fair again. Which is a good thing because in later years I may have had more than $14 in my wallet. I have also successfully steered clear of casinos, lotteries, and big-stake poker games. And I also saved a lot of time and agony by politely hanging up the phone on phone solicitors and immediately dropping junk mail in the trash. I may have lost my big chance to win a free Caribbean vacation or a jackpot worth millions. But I don't think that was God's plan for me anyway. So he's probably the one I should be thanking.

Checking the List

I'm a smart guy, just like you. But I also recognize that I can still be fooled. In Matthew 24:24, Jesus warns that much more is at stake than a few bucks in our wallets and bank accounts. Satan's deceivers are after our souls. "False messiahs and false prophets will appear and perform great signs and wonders to deceive, if possible, even the elect." Indeed, Satan is sneakier and smarter than you and me. Thankfully, we can call anytime on the name of Jesus, and he will rescue us, allowing us to claim ultimate victory.

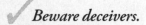 *Beware deceivers.*

Get Out of Hot Water

B ack in the 1980s, I worked for Matthew Bender & Company as a traveling salesman. My product was high-end law books with bindings that could be updated as laws changed, courts ruled, and experts commented. My clients were in-house attorneys for corporations large enough to have in-house attorneys. My territory included parts of Illinois, Indiana, Wisconsin, and Iowa.

I can look back now and see how God used that experience in my life, but certainly those two years were sadly lacking in terms of meeting financial goals and achieving personal fulfillment. I was not a good salesman.

Some days, I'd take the commuter train into Chicago and schlep my 28-pound leather briefcase up and down elevators to oak-paneled offices with floor-to-ceiling windows. Some days I'd drive our only car to the far reaches of my sales territory, staying overnight in one of those midpriced motel rooms with names like Red Roof Inn, Best Western, and Howard Johnson.

I lasted only a couple years as a traveling sales rep, but I totally honor those road warriors of a generation ago. Even if you were good at it, the never-ending pressure took its toll. The only thing worse than the impossible monthly sales quotas was the steady stream of lonely dinners and sagging mattresses.

One desperately cold night as I entered my motel room, I stomped the slush off my wingtips and was initially glad to feel the rush of warmth from the motel furnace. But it wasn't long before the over-heated and dry air left me gasping for breath. The motel heating system clearly didn't have a humidifier. That's when this clever boy had the brilliant idea to run a hot shower at full blast to fill the room and fill my lungs with a comforting fog of steam. It worked! And I fell asleep.

I woke six or seven hours later to two sounds. My alarm clock. And running water. Cold water.

I felt a little bad wasting all that water. I felt worse when I couldn't take a hot shower to start my day. And I felt even worse when I checked out. I discovered several of my fellow travelers giving quite an earful to the beleaguered desk clerk. He certainly couldn't explain why the entire establishment had run out of hot water. It had never happened before.

I briefly considered offering an apology and an explanation. Instead, I paid my bill quietly and hit the road.

If you were in that unnamed motel in that unnamed Midwestern state on that winter night decades ago, I truly apologize. I don't think it would have done any good for me to have confessed in front of that angry mob of weary, cold-showered travelers. Probably the hotel management would have liked to know what caused the hot-water shortage. But by leaving quietly, I saved them from having to file a police report on the lynching that most certainly would have taken place on their property.

As I type this, I feel better already. Confessing my cowardice and self-centered act to the world has lifted a burden from my heart. My actions were not malicious, but they did bring discomfort to more than few travelers and motel employees. At this point I would like to apologize face-to-face to all involved, but that's an impossibility. Admittedly, the story has an element of dark humor. But it still was an unpleasant experience for many, and I was to blame.

How about you? Might there be an inadvertent misstep from long ago that has left some lingering guilt? As a child did you pick some roses for your mom, not realizing they were being fertilized and pruned by a neighbor for an upcoming flower show? Did you innocently write your name in wet cement, only to watch city workers jackhammer that section of sidewalk and replace it days later? At your place of work, did you receive primary kudos for a successful project in which you were barely involved? Looking over your supermarket receipt at home, did you realize you never paid for the bag of dog food in the lower rack of the shopping cart?

In the moment, it's always best to confess. But if it's been weeks or decades, it's probably time to let it go. Maybe the best idea now is to somehow pay it forward. (Or since we're talking about a past misdeed, maybe a better term is "pay it backward.") In other words, consider your crime and imagine some corresponding atonement or reparation.

If you're guilty of picking the neighbor's roses as a child, take a bouquet of flowers to a senior shut-in this week. If you defaced some cement work, shovel your neighbor's sidewalk and driveway this winter. If you took credit for someone else's hard work, write a note of appreciation to an old boss or mentor. If you accidentally stole a bag of dog food, spend a day volunteering at the local animal shelter.

You get the idea. We all make mistakes. And God really doesn't want us dragging around a sackful of guilt and shame. Let's fix all the shortcomings we can. Let's confess and willingly face the consequences for our major mess-ups. But for the small stuff from long ago that nags our conscience, let's turn negatives into positives.

Anticipate and be grateful for the leading of the Holy Spirit. When the Spirit convicts you of something you need to make right, don't be surprised if an opportunity comes along before you know it.

Maybe that explains why I felt pretty good when I had a chance to donate to build clean water wells in western Africa. It was God's way of reminding me that I can't maneuver through this world without him.

Checking the List

Don't beat yourself up over silly, innocent mistakes from the past. Instead, turn your shortcomings over to God. He can make all things new. He can turn a negative into a positive. He doesn't need your help, but he just might allow you to be an active part in the recovery process.

When presented with an opportunity to do something nice, check your motivation. If you're doing it for your own glory, that's fine. You may certainly go ahead with the project. Many worthwhile endeavors are completed for less than noble reasons. But following God's lead and checking items off a heavenly bucket list—maybe even anonymously—will deliver a fresh joy and personal satisfaction that only a true believer can know.

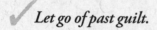 *Let go of past guilt.*

Practice Your Penmanship

Remember back in high school when you practiced your autograph? I'm well aware that schools don't teach penmanship in second and third grade anymore. You can prove that by looking at the handwriting of most middle and high school students. It's usually a weird combination of printing and cursive, capital and lowercase. School administrators apparently feel classroom time is better spent on keyboarding skills. They're probably right.

I remember intentionally changing my signature my junior year of high school. The first letter of my first name is *J*, and traditionally that includes a large loop on top and smaller loop below. For several years, my signature had a high loop that ended with a straight line below. But one day—without considering that a signature is used for identification purposes—I changed it. For whatever reason, I decided the *J* looked cooler beginning with a straight line swooping down and ending with a large loop below the line. Hey, it's my signature. Unfortunately, a bank teller didn't see it that way and wouldn't cash my check until I came back with two other forms of identification.

Wouldn't it be wonderful if you could reinvent yourself as easily as you can reinvent your signature? Well, you can. But you can't do it alone. It takes a four-way partnership. The Father loving us unconditionally and offering each of us the free gift of grace through his Son. Jesus demonstrating a perfect life and taking the punishment for our sins. The Holy Spirit filling and leading us. And finally, our own decision to accept the gift and pursue a life that gives glory back to God. The Bible teaches that "anyone who belongs to Christ has become a new person. The old life is gone; a new life has begun!" (2 Corinthians 5:17 NLT). That's even more life changing than a new signature.

Is it easy? Well, maybe not. You've got to come to a place of surrender, and that's not something most people want to do. But the change is very real. You probably won't see it in the mirror, and many of your old habits will still linger. But new you are. What's more, your name is then written in the book of life and cannot be erased.

At a recent book-signing event, more than a hundred people lined up for one of my books and an autograph. Again and again, I scrawled my name with all the appropriate loops and swirls, adding a pithy statement inside each front cover. Only afterward did I stop to consider what had transpired. Superficially, marking each book with a felt-tipped pen felt like defacing a piece of property. But actually, each signature signified a transfer of ownership. From my hand to theirs. To complete the analogy, that's what happens when you give your life to Christ. He owns it. Which is a very good thing. Because his plan for your life far exceeds anything you could imagine or achieve on your own.

Checking the List

Make sure your name is written in permanent ink in the book of life. Only God can inscribe your name in that book, but it's still a choice you must make yourself. So your penmanship is not nearly as important as your decision to put Christ first.

Once you do understand grace and accept the gift, it's a done deal. You only have to scratch that item off God's bucket list for your life one time, although ongoing celebration is in order: "Rejoice that your names are recorded in heaven" (Luke 10:20 NLT).

Still, as long as there is breath in your body, there's much work ahead. Yes, your sins have been forgiven and even forgotten in heaven. But here on earth, there are still consequences and ramifications for sins of the past and the future. But take heart. Earthly suffering is temporary. The glory of eternity awaits.

Well worth noting: Eternity is not pretty for those who deny God or believe their good deeds will earn them a place in heaven. "Anyone whose name was not found written in the book of life was thrown into the lake of fire" (Revelation 20:15).

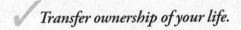 ***Transfer ownership of your life.***

Live Grudge-Free

I'm carrying grudges against about five people right now. (1) Someone I barely knew from college who spread some nasty lies and rumors about me. (2) A former coach of one my kids' teams who made some really poor choices. (3) A work colleague whose stubbornness cost me thousands of dollars. (4-5) Two others I can't talk about.

To be clear, I don't wish these five guys any real harm. Let's just say I wouldn't mind if they developed some kind of recurring discomfort. Maybe a hangnail that comes back every couple weeks. Or a check-engine light that flashes once in a while for no reason at all. If they suffered an annual bout with jock itch, pinkeye, or head lice, part of me thinks that would make me very happy.

But you and I both know it doesn't work that way.

Actually, I'm embarrassed and dismayed that such thoughts would enter my head. Really I'm a nice guy. Just like you. And I would not receive any real joy from the discomfort of others.

Interesting thing about grudges—they have a greater negative impact on the grudge holder than the grudge target. A researcher at Duke University, John Barefoot, explored the relationship between hostility and physical health. He followed up on a group of doctors and lawyers who had taken personality profiles 25 years earlier in med school and law school. Doctors who ranked in the more hostile half of their class had a cardiac death rate almost five times as high as their classmates. Lawyers who ranked in the top one-quarter of the hostility scale were four times as likely to have died than those in the bottom quarter. Barefoot confirmed three aspects of hostility were particularly unhealthy—cynicism, hostile feelings, and a tendency to respond with aggression.[6]

Really, that's not surprising. Our mothers have been telling us for years to play nice and not store up resentment. You can almost hear a grandmother's shaky voice saying, "You gotta let go of those bad feelings, otherwise they just eat at ya."

So if grudges don't bring us satisfaction and may be dangerous to our health, why do we hang on to them so tightly? Maybe we're waiting and hoping for some kind of apology. Well, here's more news for you. That's not going to happen.

I'm convinced that most people who do us wrong either don't know or don't care. Which means an apology is the last thing to expect. We're the ones who suffer while the individual who ticked us off feels no pain. The late great comedic actor Buddy Hackett had some valuable insight on the subject: "I've had a few arguments with people, but I never carry a grudge. You know why? While you're carrying a grudge, they're out dancing."

Finally, if we were really honest with ourselves, we would admit we should simply let the other person off the hook. When they did you wrong, they may have been in a high-stress situation that leaves them with a reasonable excuse. For instance, anything screamed by a new mom in a delivery room should not be taken personally by the new dad. If you're holding a grudge against a bride for something she did on the day of her wedding, let it go. When flashing lights from a squad car appear in a rearview mirror, a passenger should not be judgmental about the next words out of the driver's mouth. Also, be extra understanding about anything spoken at emotionally charged locations, such as emergency rooms, youth sporting events, and funeral homes.

Scratching off this item from your bucket list is quite freeing. Grudges are joy killers and major burdens. It's pretty difficult to smile when excess bile is eating away at your stomach lining. And even though there's no scientific proof, it probably takes a lot more energy to hold a grudge than to let it go.

I must admit, just writing this chapter has been wonderfully cathartic. And productive. I hereby announce my list of currently held grudges is now officially down to…two. Or maybe three.

Checking the List

If you are currently holding a grudge, it's your choice to keep it or drop it. If you hang on to it, the repercussions can be significant even beyond this world. In James 5:9, the Bible teaches that the individual holding the grudge is more likely to be judged: "Don't grumble against one another, brothers and sisters, or you will be judged." With that in mind, dumping every grudge makes even more sense, doesn't it?

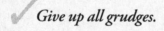 *Give up all grudges.*

Take Note of Any Quick Fix

Every spring, the school secretary would call my classmate Marlene and me out of class and march us down to the teacher's lounge for speech testing. Marlene had a lisp of sorts. And I couldn't say my *r*'s.

The state-mandated speech therapist would flip through some illustrated flash cards, and I would dutifully say "wooster" and "bawn" instead of "rooster" and "barn." As though she were learning something new, the speech expert would make lengthy notes on her clipboard before Marlene and I were escorted back to class. A month later the report would come back with the not-so-surprising news, "Jay has difficulty saying words containing the letter *r*." To me, the annual review of my obvious flaw was a little humiliating and clearly unproductive.

When I was 12, my family moved to a neighboring town, and I started at a new school. Once again, I went to a special room for speech testing, dutifully identified similar flash cards, and then hustled back to class. But someone in some office in some faraway building decided to take an additional step. Within a week, I began to meet with a speech therapist. In our very first session, she taught me to move my tongue back against the roof of my mouth when talking about roosters, rabbits, barns, and horses. Problem solved. We kept meeting once a week for a couple months so I could practice, but really the fix was instantaneous.

I remember becoming more and more self-conscious about my speech impediment. When you're in kindergarten or younger, a slight lisp or sloppy pronunciations might be considered cute. But as you approach middle school, the inability to speak clearly with your peers can shatter your confidence. No preteen wants to be saying "besketti" or "birfday."

It wasn't until decades later that I realized how important it was that my dysfunction had been identified and remedied. Today, I regularly do radio and TV interviews, speak in front of thousands of people, and even record voiceover narrations and audiobooks. The ability to accurately pronounce words with *r*'s is a necessary skill. And I can't help but wonder how my life would have been different without that quick fix when I was in seventh grade.

I also can't help but wonder how many other very real shortcomings in our lives God has alleviated with minimal fuss, opening the door for us to better serve him.

It's absolutely true that God allows hardships and crises in our lives to purify us, prepare us for battle, and confirm our dependence on him. But that's an entirely different topic. This chapter flips that idea upside down by asking, what obstacles has God *already removed* from your life so you can forge ahead and do great things?

Have you endured a disease or affliction that is now quite treatable but would have severely limited your abilities had you been born a few decades earlier?

Did a mentor, teacher, pastor, or hobbyist just happen to enter your life at just the right moment, helping you discover a hidden talent that would otherwise have gone untapped?

Were you painfully shy until someone in authority forced you out of your comfort zone so you could discover you had a voice and something worth saying?

Did you go to a doctor for a minor ailment and just by sheer luck uncover another much more severe medical problem that was successfully treated only because you caught it in the early stages?

Maybe every member of your family for generations had to overcome a burden, but circumstances have changed and now you don't have to. Maybe you're first in your family who learned to read. Maybe you're the first generation to live in a country where you're free to be anything you want to be. Maybe your hardworking parents lifted your family out of poverty, and suddenly you don't have to worry about your next meal. Maybe you were exposed to the Bible at an early age and did not have to unlearn the baggage of religions that worship false gods or overlook the power of grace.

Please don't take any of this for granted. If you were on the receiving end of walls that came down quickly, you may be well-prepared to step out and answer God's call sooner than most.

Oh, to be sure, there will be walls you will need to bash through. But take a moment now to assess any areas you have mastered because of a quick fix. You might be surprised to find those exact skills and capabilities are desperately needed for a project that's right in front of you. Or right around the corner.

I haven't seen Marlene in more than four decades. I hope she also found a quick-and-easy fix and is using her gifts to serve others.

Checking the List

One of the most important questions we can ask is, "What has God done in my life, and how can I give that gift back to him?" First Peter 4:10 confirms, "Each of you should use whatever gift you have received to serve others, as faithful stewards of God's grace."

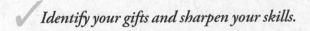 *Identify your gifts and sharpen your skills.*

Kill 'Em with Kindness

By now you're getting the sense that the plan for completing God's bucket list is counterintuitive to what the world suggests. When the culture says "more," God would usually say "less." When the world says, "Elbow your way to the front of the line," Jesus reveals, "The first shall be last."

We can imagine the Pharisees mocking the widow for putting a meager two pennies in the offering plate. Much to their surprise, Jesus praises the woman for quietly giving everything she had. The Beatitudes are filled with ideas that clash with worldly values. We could fill this book with other examples.

But the difference between God's way and the world's way is never more striking than when it comes to the concept of revenge. Society tends to follow the Old Testament injunction, "Eye for eye, tooth for tooth" (Exodus 21:24). Jesus says, "Turn the other cheek" (Matthew 5:38-39).

How does that idea sound? I don't know how many enemies you have, but Jesus of Nazareth had quite a few. When the time came for his arrest, scourging, and crucifixion, once again he demonstrated the power of forgiveness. His last words on the cross included these: "Father, forgive them, for they do not know what they are doing" (Luke 23:34).

Is that ability in you? Consider for a moment any men, women, boys, or girls who have done you wrong. From work, your community, or perhaps even your family. There's no need to get graphic or specific here. But you may have endured great harm physically, emotionally, or spiritually.

If the very thought of these people causes you to imagine opportunities for revenge, please don't beat yourself up. (And I apologize for stirring those memories.) It's human to want to get even when we've been belittled, assaulted, ridiculed, mocked, scorned, bullied, robbed, or harassed. Our desire for revenge is even more natural if someone we love has been violated.

Yes, it's natural. But it's also wrong. That's why we need a *supernatural* response. Under our own power, there's no way we can live up to the command, "Love your enemies and pray for those who persecute you."

Does that clear command from Matthew 5:44 sound impossible? It may well be for nonbelievers. But those who trust God can count on the Holy Spirit to guide them. We can actually love our persecutors the same way God loves them. We can pray for them because we know God's intervention really can soften their hearts—and ours.

Beyond that, allow me to add a couple biblical principles that may make this idea of loving your enemies a little more manageable. First, you can be sure they are not getting away with anything. Your enemies will have to settle up with God at a later date. Second, there is a way to utilize their malevolent nature to turn their life around. And, friend, you just might be the right person for the job. Here's the strategy: Kill 'em with kindness.

> Do not repay anyone evil for evil. Be careful to do what
> is right in the eyes of everyone. If it is possible, as far as it
> depends on you, live at peace with everyone. Do not take
> revenge, my dear friends, but leave room for God's wrath,
> for it is written: "It is mine to avenge; I will repay," says
> the Lord. On the contrary:

"If your enemy is hungry, feed him;
if he is thirsty, give him something to drink.
In doing this, you will heap burning coals on his head."
Do not be overcome by evil, but overcome evil with good
(Romans 12.17-21).

What a brilliant concept. Treat your persecutor with dignity. Meet their needs, respond with grace, and your actions may shine light into their dark heart for the very first time. Your sincere love, reluctant though it is, may open their eyes to how they've been acting and to the damage they've done. There's a good chance they have wronged others as well, and just about everyone they know is an enemy. Suddenly you come along and treat them with unconditional love and respect. Without a doubt, your display of grace will get their attention. (Almost as if you've dumped hot coals on their head!) Your act of kindness may have an impact on their family for generations to come.

It may be hard to admit, but God loves your persecutors just as much as he loves you. It would be nice to be his favorite, but that's not the way it works. Besides, we are all far from perfect. We mess up all the time. That's the sinful nature of man.

Which takes us back to the Lord's Prayer, in which we ask God, "Forgive us our debts, as we also have forgiven our debtors." In other words, if we really want to get right with God, we probably have to reduce our revenge-seeking and any long-standing animosity by about 100 percent.

While you're working on that, look around and see if anyone is trying to get your attention by dumping a few hot coals on your head.

Checking the List

You've been wronged. And it would be real nice if the culprit broke down sobbing and begged your forgiveness. But let's face it, that doesn't happen very often. Even without tears or drama, straightforward apologies are rare occurrences. Which means you are responsible only for your side of the forgiveness equation. You can't wipe clean the other person's sin. But you can turn to God for strength, ask him to remove your bitterness, and come out of the darkness. If God chooses to bless you with a dose of supernatural strength, you might even have a chance to express love to the person who wronged you. Can you imagine that?

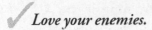 *Love your enemies.*

Uncover Secrets of Generations Past

The year I was born, my mom's parents moved from Beloit, Wisconsin, to Albuquerque, New Mexico, for a secret government job. The year was 1957, and the nuclear arms race was coming of age. No one in the family, not even Grandma, knew what Orlando Mauel did. Fifteen years earlier, the supersecret lab at nearby Los Alamos had been ground zero for research for the Manhattan Project, the Allied effort to produce the atomic weapons that effectively ended World War II. Family lore suggests that Grandpa Mauel worked at Sandia National Laboratories, a branch of Los Alamos.

Setting aside for a moment any controversy about nuclear power and government secrets, it's cool to consider the secret lives of our recent ancestors. Not our parents. We know too much about them. But take a moment to consider the exploits and adventures of your grandparents, great-aunts and uncles, or even great-grandparents. Most of us have some memories of those generations, albeit clouded by images of their gray hair, slow-moving joints, and recently discovered personas as retirees.

Plus, anytime you were with your grandparents, they were, by definition, grandparents. Hard-charging CEOs, gruff steelworkers, disciplined operating-room nurses, and gritty journalists all turn to mush when they hold their grandbabies. In other words, most people wouldn't even recognize their grandparents at the peak of their productive years. Find a black-and-white photo of your granny or granddad on the job, and you won't recognize the look in their eyes.

All of which opens our imagination to who they were and what they accomplished. Let's play that game for a moment. Consider what you know for sure about your grandparents, and throw out any negative baggage. Spin a yarn that paints Meemaw and Papa in the absolute best light. Were they the first of their family to graduate, own a home, or launch a business? Did they move across the globe or country to start a new life? Were they more engineer or artist? What role did God play in their lives? Were they motivated by fame, fortune, or family? Did they own any patents, play any instruments, run for office, or serve as church elders? Were they bobby-soxers in the 1940s, beatniks in the '50s, or hippies in the '60s? What did they read, watch, write, play, sing, build, buy, and sell? What kind of things were on their bucket lists?

If Gram or Gramps is around, ask them. You might learn something. There's a reason the Bible tells us, "Stand up in the presence of the elderly, and show respect for the aged" (Leviticus 19:32 NLT).

Internet research and websites like ancestry.com can augment and prompt memories from older relatives. "What do you remember about your Aunt Dorothy who grew up in Yonkers?" is a more engaging question than "Tell me about your relatives."

In my youth, third- or fourth-grade students often tackled the popular "family tree" assignment with enthusiasm. Entire extended families would get involved in sharing memories of long-gone relatives, unusual jobs, memorable neighborhoods, and anecdotes, including some that had never been passed on. Those homework assignments are no longer as common. An increase in divorce, single parenthood, advanced reproductive technology, and alternative lifestyles has led some educators to reevaluate that curriculum, according to the *New York Times*.

The most entrenched and problematic of these assignments, teachers, school administrators and psychologists said, is the classic family tree, which requires pupils to trace maternal and paternal ancestral lines...

Some educators have reacted to the evolving family constellations by scrapping the family tree altogether, while others...have modified it. Teachers now assign family time lines, family orchards and essays that give children more freedom in telling their personal histories.[7]

Such changes in our schools and culture remind us of an even greater need today for families to be intentional about reviving the art of conversation—at dinner tables, on porches, around fireplaces, and strolling down gravel roads. That's how life, history, dreams, and faith are best shared.

These commandments that I give you today are to be on your hearts. Impress them on your children. Talk about them when you sit at home and when you walk along the road, when you lie down and when you get up (Deuteronomy 6:6-7).

Personally, I'll always be glad for my daughter's assignment to interview a relative. Rae Anne captured some audio of my dad sharing stories of World War II he had never mentioned before. It's a cherished recording. On one of my own grandmother's last Thanksgiving meals at my home, I spurred her to share some memories. Knowing she was born in 1900, I asked about the first time she saw an airplane. Her face lit up as she recalled hanging laundry in her backyard with her mom and being awestruck at the sight of a biplane overhead.

A friendly reminder. Conversations like these need to happen sooner rather than later.

To finish that nudge, allow me to give you a three-part assignment. First, if you have any grandparents still with us, make a point to follow through even *before* the next family holiday. Second, if that generation has passed on, ask your own parents about their parents. Encourage them to move beyond superficial memories. If it's painful, don't push it. But you may well be initiating the best conversation you have all year. Finally, share a few amusing or engaging things you remember about your grandparents or parents with a few members of the youngest generation in your family. Keep it mostly positive, winsome, and filled with hope.

Checking the List

We have a responsibility to preserve our family history and honor the contributions of our ancestors. Often, proud parents will go overboard extolling the accomplishments of the youngest family members while Grandma and Grampa nod and applaud. That's not a bad thing. Grandparents love to brag about their grandkids. But let's make sure the entire family listens with love as living history gets passed down.

Celebrating traditions and sharing life-changing moments unites families and keeps them strong. Psalm 145:4 says, "One generation commends your works to another; they tell of your mighty acts." Have you ever asked your parents or grandparents how and when they have seen God work in their lives?

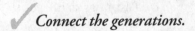 *Connect the generations.*

Make Sure You're Missed

The previous chapter was about your responsibility to reach back into the past to make sure the heritage of your parents and their parents is not forgotten. This chapter is about your legacy. It's especially important if you're a parent or you have young kids in your life.

I didn't cry at my grandfather's funeral. He was 78. I was a junior in college.

I grew up in the Chicago suburbs, about two hours from where Nana and Grandpa lived, and I probably saw them four or five times a year. My family would drive up to Racine, Wisconsin, for Christmas, Thanksgiving, and Easter. Occasionally they would drive down, but the visits were short and not memorable. Maybe they weren't comfortable spending the night. Maybe they had better things to do.

Doing the math, over my first 20 years of life I would have had about 100 chances to interact with my father's parents. All the short visits, at our house or theirs, were stiff and pretty much uncomfortable. But every year in early August we would spend an entire week with them up at Pine Lake in northern Wisconsin. Those days were not awkwardly stiff at all—they were filled with catching fish, gutting fish, eating fish, swimming, hiking, playing family-friendly games, and sitting around the fireplace in the big cabin that held about a dozen members of my extended family. All solid memories.

Going "up north" for extended time with Nana and Grandpa gave me a taste of what a relationship between kids and grandparents could be. But only a taste. That wonderful annual experience on the lake still did not create enough closeness to stir any true depth of feeling for Grandpa Fritz when he passed away. I didn't really know the man. And vice versa. At the time, I didn't realize what I had missed. I also will never know if Grandpa Fritz had any regrets.

Standing in dramatic contrast is the wake and funeral service of my own father just four years ago. In front of a roomful of mourners, my four sons each spent a few minutes sharing heartfelt personal memories of time spent with Papa. The words spoken by Alec, Randall, Max, and Isaac all reflected the intimate relationship they had with my dad, of which even I was jealous. The funeral parlor and church overflowed with laughter and weeping. While they spoke, all four young men had to stop more than once to gather their composure and brush back streaming tears. It was a beautiful thing. It was a tribute to what the relationship between grandparents and grandkids can be.

How do relationships like that happen? Well, it's not by accident. I can look back and discern three specific decisions that led to the incomparable bond between my dad and my kids. At the time, we didn't realize the full magnitude of those life choices.

One of my first memories of my own fatherhood was visiting my parents with our firstborn, Alec, when he was just a few weeks old. Rita and I had been trying to figure out if she would be able to be the best mom in the world and also juggle some kind of income-producing career. Sitting in my parents' kitchen, I broached the topic of their availability as babysitters.

My dad, who clearly loved Alec more than anything in the world, took a moment to consider the magnitude of the request. Finally he said, "We will be there for anything you need. Anytime, anyplace. But please, let's not intentionally create a situation in which our grandson is a burden to us."

In the moment, my dad's reply felt a bit harsh. But we soon realized it was brilliant.

Those words led to a critical early decision for Rita and me in our role as parents. Our children would deliver only joy to their grandparents. We would never guilt them into babysitting. We would never complain to them about our kids. In all communication, we would put a positive spin on all aspects of life as we added three more sons and a daughter. Rita and I didn't live in denial. Our five children were typical kids with all the typical kid challenges. We knew that if a crisis arose, my parents would heroically step up and fill in any gap. But as our family grew, we learned to handle the routine ups and downs of raising a family and trust God that it would all work out for good. A funny thing happens when you start looking for the joys in life. They tend to come around more and more often. As it turns out, my dad's bold statement made me a better father. This was my family, and the responsibility was mine.

The second critical decision that led to an awesome relationship between my kids and my folks is that we never moved away. I fully realize that many young families are moving across the country for career advancement or perhaps to *escape* their extended family. If you feel the need to move some distance away to keep your sanity or safety, that's an entirely different issue that I won't address here. But before you move away to advance your career, think long and hard about how that will impact your family relationships. Not pursuing job opportunities in Grand Rapids, Seattle, and Dallas were some of the best decisions I ever made.

Fortunately, Papa and Mimi never moved either. I don't think it was ever considered, even during the snowiest winter or hottest summer. The fact that they had 11 grandkids within six miles may have had something to do with it.

We've seen firsthand the very real benefits of kids living near their grandparents. Applause doubles at concerts, recitals, and soccer games. Grandparents who live in town read the same local paper and drive down the same streets. That means two more people who love your kids as much as you do are on constant lookout for opportunities, events, distractions, and dangers. Plus, there's a serendipitous give-and-take. Lawns get mowed. Cookies get made. Life gets shared. Cousins get to really know each other. Mommies and daddies can get away for a weekend. And some lucky kids even get to run errands with Grandpa.

Which brings us to the third critical decision. My 60-year-old dad did not go out and buy a red Corvette to help him feel young again. He bought a minivan with lots of seat belts so he could take a pile of grandkids anytime, anyplace. Which, in turn, made him feel young again. I'm convinced that was a choice he made specifically because he had grandkids in town that were a joy, not a burden. Worth noting, he pretty much never took the kids to the zoo or amusement park. Instead, they'd go on routine trips to the supermarket or hardware store, or maybe shopping for school supplies. Papa's minivan might stop to get ice cream or feed the ducks, but it was always an adventure found in everyday life. He called it "bumming with Papa," and it might be his greatest legacy.

So those are three decisions that opened the floodgates to a bucket of tears at my dad's funeral. In review, for those parents who want to foster that same kind of relationship between the previous and the next generations, here they are again.

- Choose to make your kids a joy to the extended family, not a burden.
- Choose to build your life nearby.
- Choose to build relationships during the course of real life, not once-a-year extravaganzas.

In twenty-first-century America, the family seems to be less of a priority. But I believe a few wise choices can go a long way toward keeping our extended families together. This author has recently been thinking long and hard about that idea. You see, my first *three* grandchildren were born while I was working on this book.

Checking the List

We have a responsibility to the young people in our lives. And to our parents. Whether you're a mother, father, aunt, uncle, neighbor, or friend. We need to tell tales and share histories. We need to listen with love and speak with vibrancy. In the Old Testament, King Hezekiah describes how giving praise to God in the moment leads to a faith that endures from generation to generation: "The living, the living—they praise you, as I am doing today; parents tell their children about your faithfulness" (Isaiah 38:19). Have you seen God work in your life? Tell the next generation. And the next. And the next.

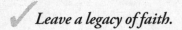 *Leave a legacy of faith.*

Do Typical Bucket-List Stuff

With this chapter, we're halfway through God's bucket list as I've imagined it. Some readers may have given up. But my sincere thanks to you for staying the course—even if you remain skeptical about the entire premise.

A little skepticism is to be expected because we're pretending to have a handle on how God thinks. (And that's just silly.) Also, the list we're compiling doesn't feel like a traditional bucket list. Most of these chapters seem to be more about abstract concepts than specific places to go, things to do, and events to attend.

So to keep everybody happy, let's set aside the next few pages to assemble a more obvious bucket list for men and women who really do want to pursue God's will. Some items are obvious. Some not so much. The possibilities are endless, but let's try to focus on goals we really can achieve.

Volunteer in a soup kitchen for the homeless. Do this. With friends or family members. It's hands-on. It's eye-opening. And there's probably a homeless shelter not too far from your home address. Ladling soup, pouring coffee, and chatting with guests puts you in the trenches doing work that meets a real need. It's an excellent introduction to developing the heart of a servant. I recommend scheduling yourself on days that are not holidays.

Read the entire Bible in a year. Some people do this every year. Reading schedules are readily available. Several publishers produce Bibles conveniently divided into 365 readings. If that's too intimidating, give yourself two years. Or three. Or five.

Go on a short-term mission trip. Journey to a foreign land or an underserved area of the United States to build a church, repair homes, perform medical services, encourage pastors, visit prisoners, or spend time with eager, smiling children. In many cases, the most important aspect of the trip is your foray out of your comfort zone. Look for short-term mission opportunities that *don't* feel like vacations.

Stand on the rim of the Grand Canyon. No one can do this and not think about God. That's why it's on the list.

Do sidewalk counseling outside a Planned Parenthood clinic. According to their own annual report, Planned Parenthood performs more than 300,000 abortions per year. When volunteer counselors share messages of love and offer prayers for women about to enter those clinics, sometimes babies are saved. Sounds like a noble cause to me.

Attend a sing-along Messiah *at Christmastime.* Every December in Chicago and other cities around the world, professional musicians join with everyday music lovers to perform the moving masterpiece of George Frideric Handel. If the organizers don't sell copies of the vocal score, you can order yours online.

Look up in the Sistine Chapel. History, religion, art, architecture, church politics, and so much more come together in this iconic structure in Vatican City. Imagine Michelangelo and his colleagues investing four years of their lives during the first part of the sixteenth century creating the magnificent frescoes that adorn the ceiling.

Visit the Holy Land. Walk where Jesus walked. Bethlehem. Nazareth. Jerusalem. The Sea of Galilee. The Garden of Gethsemane. The Mount of Olives. Golgotha. The term "life changing" is used way too often to describe a variety of events and experiences. But standing in Israel and recalling the well-documented events of Christ's life truly is.

Drop a huge anonymous gift in a Salvation Army bucket. If it's a true sacrificial gift, you'll feel great. Don't blow it by telling someone!

Start a conversation with a stranger about spiritual things. The best way to really test your own belief system is to present it thoughtfully and perhaps boldly to a stranger. If it gets a little heated, that's not always bad. Next time, you'll be even better prepared.

Spend a week in solitude. Would a week by yourself without speaking drive you bonkers? That monastic experience—just you and God—could actually be a turning point for your life.

Deliver an Angel Tree gift. Present a Christmas gift to the child of a prison inmate and let them know they have not been forgotten by their mommy or daddy. Every year, this ministry of Prison Fellowship delivers hope to children, helps reconnect families, and softens the hearts of inmates who can't believe that someone actually cares about their lives and their children. All in the name of Jesus.

Chaperone a church youth event. High school. Middle school. Or even younger. Surrender your adult instincts and enjoy the experience. Stay positive, and you may even have a life-changing conversation with some young man or woman who needs some direction only you can give. It may be your ministry sweet spot! Or not.

Attend a stadium evangelistic event. Millions have come to Christ at crusades featuring Billy Graham and other powerful and sincere preachers. Salvation decisions are made individually, but sometimes thousands come forward at a single event. Unforgettable.

Read these six Christian classics.

In His Steps by Charles Sheldon
More Than a Carpenter by Josh McDowell
The Screwtape Letters by C.S. Lewis
Through the Gates of Splendor by Elisabeth Elliot
The Pilgrim's Progress by John Bunyan
Knowing God by J.I. Packer

Bookmark this page and check these items off one by one over the next 36 months. When you finish, track me down at my website—jaypayleitner.com—and let me know. Or even better, invite me to join you as you ceremoniously check off the last item. But be warned, I'm going to ask you how you're doing on the other 51 items in this book!

Checking the List

This is as good a time as any to remember that we need to be more than deep thinkers and big talkers. We need to be doers of the Word. In Matthew 7:21, Jesus said, "Not everyone who says to me, 'Lord, Lord,' will enter the kingdom of heaven, but only the one who does the will of my Father who is in heaven."

 *Go, do, and live like you believe.*

Peek into Dark Corners

There's another checklist that might belong on God's bucket list. It's imagining yourself walking through every room in your home and surrendering it to Christ. But more than just giving him control over a room, the idea is to yield related parts of your life. That personal inventory might sound something like this.

> Welcome, Jesus, into my home and my heart. I invite you into my living room, surrendering my relationship with my family. I invite you into my kitchen, surrendering my gluttony or other bad habits related to my physical self. I invite you into my workshop, that I may use my hands to serve you. I invite you into the master bedroom, that I may trust you with my hopes and dreams and, if called to marry, that I be an affirming, unselfish spouse. I invite you into my garage, asking you to accompany me wherever I go, protecting my travels...

Using your home as a guide, you'll cover just about every area of your life as you welcome Jesus into your library, office, backyard, driveway, dining room, guest room, and so on. And for the most part, this is an easy exercise. That is, until you get to that one dark closet into which Jesus is not invited. You know the one. It's a creepy, secret place. One you're not proud of. But still you go there on a regular basis. Or maybe it's something from your past that you think is behind you, but it really isn't.

You may have heard some version of this powerful meditation before. I've traced it to a booklet written in 1954 by Robert Boyd Munger, *My Heart—Christ's Home*. Describing the unopened hall closet, Munger writes, "There's a peculiar odor in the house. Something must be dead around here. It's upstairs. I think it's in the hall closet." The author describes an internal battle that ends in finally surrendering the key to that closet. The rotting stuff is thrown out and the closet cleaned and painted. "Immediately, a fresh, fragrant breeze swept through the house. The whole atmosphere changed. What release and victory to have that dead thing out of my life!"

The booklet finishes with an invitation to transfer the ownership of your house from your name to the name of Jesus. Once his name is on the title, you are still responsible for daily upkeep, but the foundation will never crumble, and the lights will never dim. As a matter of fact, once you give him the deed to your life, you gain a second home. That heavenly home will have no tubs to scrub or gutters to clean.

> For we know that if the earthly tent we live in is destroyed,
> we have a building from God, an eternal house in heaven,
> not built by human hands (2 Corinthians 5:1).

Whether you rent or own, go ahead and invite Jesus on a tour through every room in your life. Be especially aware of any hesitation you have as you approach each room. If you pause at a doorway before entering, that might indicate the need to spend a little extra time throwing back the curtains, looking in the dark corners, and cleaning out the cobwebs.

Checking the List

As you can imagine, when you let the light of Christ shine into every corner of your life, he's going to reveal things you've been hiding.

Maybe for years. Unpleasant things that you may not want any-one to see. The truth is, Jesus has been fully aware of your dark-est secrets from the very beginning. But he loved you anyway. And still does.

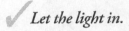 *Let the light in.*

Get Nose-to-Nose with an Alligator

Our trip to the Florida Keys began in Miami and took us along the edge of the Everglades. I saw it as the perfect chance to introduce my kids to the largest subtropical wilderness in the United States, home to all kinds of snakes, gators, and other critters. Rita, of course, thought otherwise. She had seen the pictures and heard the stories.

She was not eager for a marsh to suck one of our precious children into a bottomless sinkhole, never to be seen again. Nor did she want to ride in a bouncing swamp buggy or an airboat propelled by a giant fan. For some reason, the idea of picking swamp bugs out of our teeth or getting splashed with mucky bog water did not appeal to her. Sure, the buggies and boats supposedly came with seatbelts, but Rita could not be convinced the tour operators cared about her kids as much as she did. My bride is not a wimp, but she is wise. I respected her wishes, especially since this was the first day of our vacation.

That's how—instead of venturing into a cavern of dark, foreboding Cypress trees—we found ourselves walking safely in the sunshine along a wide, paved path that wound just a few hundred yards into a protected wetland area. (Boring.) Along one side of the path was a shallow marsh of reeds and grasses. On the other side was a man-made channel that served as a protective barrier from most of the wildlife.

Our experience felt more like an outing to a kiddie zoo than a wilderness adventure.

Strolling along, we finally saw some real live alligators on the far side of the channel. Some perhaps six feet long, they were basking in the sun, one or two slipping into the water. All of them at least 20 yards away and paying no attention to the family of tourists.

While the distant predators had our attention, seventeen-year-old Max noticed a bundle of baby alligators among the reeds just a couple feet from the pavement. The newly hatched reptiles peeking out from algae-covered water were adorable and sharable. Max could have reached out and picked up one of the babies, but he knew better. Instead, he called over his ten-year-old sister, and together they knelt at the edge of the bog and got closer and closer to the cute little creatures, which looked quite a bit like the GEICO spokeslizard.

The rest of my family was coming over to investigate when Max and Rae Anne suddenly stiffened and slowly began to back away. Right there, protecting her babies, a mama alligator lay motionless and well camouflaged. Almost entirely submerged, she was eyeing my own two children. At one point, Max's nose was less than ten inches from mama gator's nose. One false move, and Max may have lost the entire front of his face. Yikes.

We should have known. That day, Rita had already demonstrated how good moms watch out for their babies. Of course, alligator moms have the same intuition. When you see a bundle of baby gators, mama gator will not be far away.

Dear reader, your mom also came equipped with that same built-in maternal radar and protect-my-babies-at-all-cost instinct. Even if you moved out years ago, you still remember the way she worried about you, cared for your sniffles, made sure you ate your broccoli, reminded you to do your homework, and warned you about stranger danger. All rooted in a solid foundation of love and God-given maternal instinct.

So the surprising bucket list item for this chapter is this. Thank your mom. Thank her for all she did, and thank her for all she tried to do even though you didn't listen.

If she's still around, set this book down and give her call. If she's passed on, offer a prayer of thanks to God for the gift of moms. Even if your mother wasn't the best mom in the world, you know she always had your best interest in mind. So maybe it's time to move to a new era in your relationship. Just make sure it includes an extra helping of appreciation.

Even though you're all grown up, I'm betting your mom's voice still comes to you quite often with heartfelt admonitions you need to hear. Especially warnings like "Get back from that ledge," "Leave that dog alone," "Don't eat that mushroom," "Watch out for that school bus," and "Don't pick up the baby alligators."

Checking the List

God knew that sometimes we ignore his voice. That's why he created mothers.

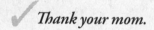 *Thank your mom.*

Dredge Up Mud-Filled Schlitz Cans

Behind my childhood home was a small woods with a meandering creek. For several years that creek was important to my brother Mark and me. We skated on it in winter and served as its caretakers in summer. It wasn't part of our property, but it was part of our life.

At strategic crossing points, we made sure the logs and branches that formed bridges remained sturdy and accessible. At a few of the bends in the creek, a million or so tiny foam pellets from some factory upstream would regularly get hung up behind a logjam of twigs and algae. We would break up the obstructions to let the water flow clear. Over one particularly ambitious week or two, Mark and I waded into the stream, filling our sneakers with muck and filling a dozen garbage bags with refuse dredged from the creek. Mostly beer and soda cans left by teenagers from years past. Initially it was going to be a recycling project earning us two cents per can. But after our dad pointed out that recyclers had little use for rusty, mud-filled Schlitz cans, we settled on a more noble cause. Our goal was to clear and clean up a modest section of our beloved creek. I guess that made us pioneers in the environmental movement.

Our project was never really a grand or noble gesture; it was just two growing boys filling a summer. Looking back, it's easy to trivialize the effort. Two summers later, a government agency took it upon themselves to dredge that creek a little deeper and a little straighter. Their equipment trampled much of the charm out of the woods. My brother and I never spent much time back there again. It was just as well—we had moved on to bigger but not necessarily better things.

Regrets? Heck no. I don't think we learned any useful skill. There was no long-term ecological benefit. My brother and I didn't form any new bond that summer (we had shared a bedroom for more than a decade). But it was the right thing to do at the time. If you had asked us why we wanted to do it, we might have quoted George Mallory's famous reason for wanting to climb Mount Everest—"Because it's there."

The Bible puts it another way. "Whatever your hand finds to do, do it with all your might" (Ecclesiastes 9:10). That's a verse you might easily skim right over. But let's pause for a moment. For young people or anyone looking to make a difference, embracing that idea is most certainly something God wants us to do. It suggests you shouldn't wait for a boss, coach, pastor, or parent to tell you what to do and how much energy to put into it. Just look around. Opportunities surround you.

Your job is to explore. Build bridges. Clear obstacles. And wade into murky waters. Expect God to place needs and challenges right in front of you. When an opportunity arises, just do it. Meet it head-on with conviction and determination. At this moment, your next task might be wonderfully clear.

Are there dirty dishes in the sink? Does the school board need someone with a Christian worldview? Does your elderly neighbor's porch need a coat of paint? Is your daughter, niece, or little sister preparing a tea party?

Do the dishes. Run for school board. Paint the porch. Sit on a tiny chair and sip pretend tea.

And make sure you do it with all your might. Scrub that casserole dish until it gleams. Run your campaign with integrity and stand firm on issues of morality and religious freedom. Whistle while you paint. And extend your pinky properly as you sip your tea and perhaps even utilize your finest British accent as you chit-chat with the young hostess.

What task has God jotted on a bucket list and placed right in front of you? Sure, someone else may be able to do it better or faster. You could ask the government for help. You could write long-winded letters to the editor about what needs to be done. But there's something noble, instructional, mind-expanding, and liberating about allowing your sneakers to fill with mud, reaching into the muck up to your elbows, and taking matters into your own hands. One piece of trash at a time.

What are you doing with your summer? Or your weekend? Or the next ten minutes? When you find something that needs doing, do it with all your heart, mind, and strength.

Checking the List

Doing it yourself is almost always better than watching someone else do it. Benefits include hands-on experience, partnership with other doers, confidence to tackle the next challenge, and appreciation for the finished work.

Also, don't be surprised if doing a menial task right in front of you leads to a job with more responsibility and even greater rewards.

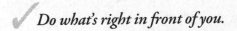 *Do what's right in front of you.*

Strive Valiantly

Not long ago my son Max caught me in a moment of hypocrisy. Let me explain.

In my college days, I was so moved by a quote from Teddy Roosevelt's "Citizen in a Republic" speech that I committed the excerpt to memory. Maybe you've seen it.

> It is not the critic who counts;
> not the man who points out how the strong man stumbles,
> or where the doer of deeds could have done them better.
> The credit belongs to the man who is actually in the arena,
> whose face is marred by dust and sweat and blood;
> who strives valiantly;
> who errs, who comes short again and again,
> because there is no effort without error and shortcoming;
> but who does actually strive to do the deeds;
> who knows the great enthusiasms, the great devotions;
> who spends himself in a worthy cause;
> who at the best knows in the end
> the triumph of high achievement,
> and who at worst, if he fails, at least fails while daring greatly,
> so that his place shall never be with those cold and timid souls
> who neither know victory nor defeat.

It's a grand little monologue and sounds even grander if recited with a slightly mocking sincerity, which just happens to be my specialty. For years, I even thought about drilling it into my children's skulls by force, but that would not have ended well. Still, they all knew it had significant meaning to me. And of course, my kids would roll their eyes on the reasonably rare occasion that I felt compelled to recite all 140 words from beginning to end.

Fortunately, several circumstances could trigger such a pontification. For instance, if I heard someone giving too much credit to a critic. Or if someone happened to mention, "dust and sweat and blood" in one sentence. Or if the topic of Teddy Roosevelt came up. Or maybe if someone was talking about great speeches or the need to memorize a paragraph for a presentation. Out of the blue, I might say, "You know, Teddy Roosevelt said, "It is not the critic who counts..." Before I got much further, the groans would come, and I would most definitely forge ahead with my unstoppable recitation.

Being forced to suffer through Dad's entire delivery of that long quote was one of our family traditions. And Max was well aware.

Max also knew that one of my *least* favorite phrases is "nice try." At a high school or youth sporting event, when an athlete makes a bone-headed blunder, a mom in the bleachers will invariably shout, "Nice try!" From my vantage point, that's like saying, "Don't worry, sweetie. It's okay. Don't think for one second that you let down your coach or team. You did the best you could, so don't concern yourself with learning from your mistake or exerting any extra effort. Just keep failing, and I'll keep cheering affirmations."

As a former coach and frequent bleacher-sitter, I have never included the words "nice try" in my vocabulary. For sure, young athletes don't want to hear those words. They want to put their fumble, terrible relay, dropped baton, or missed free throw in the past as quickly as possible. The good ones are eager for another chance to prove themselves. When Mom shouts, "Nice try," what they really hear is, "You failed."

The best option is for those in the bleachers to say nothing.

Depending on the kid, the coach might want to shout something like, "Stay focused now. Let's get it back." Or perhaps, "You'll get it next time." If the coach sees it as a teachable moment for the entire team, he may even want to call a time out. But as I've said for years, the phrase "nice try" disrespects the game and the athlete.

Now, maybe you already know where this is going and you can see what Max saw. He pointed it out to me with some amusement.

Upon further examination, the inspiring quote from Teddy Roosevelt carries *exactly* the same sentiment as "nice try." It's longer. It's more eloquent. The words are soulful and compelling. But Roosevelt was saying essentially, "Give it your best shot. If you fail, you still come out ahead." In other words, "Nice try."

Well, Max. You did it. You finally found a flaw in your old man. One of his favorite quotes and one of his least-favorite quotes are in total sync with each other. So now I've got to reconcile this dilemma. What to do, what to do?

Even I had to admit that what I think isn't nearly as important as what God might include on his bucket list for us when it comes to trying and failing. I opened my Bible.

- "Consider it pure joy, my brothers and sisters, whenever you face trials of many kinds, because you know that the testing of your faith produces perseverance" (James 1:2-3).

- In 2 Corinthians 12:9-10, Paul describes how he delights in weakness and difficulties and explains, "For when I am weak, then I am strong."

- "Though the righteous fall seven times, they rise again, but the wicked stumble when calamity strikes" (Proverbs 24:16).

So trials are good things. We find strength when we acknowledge our shortcomings. And those who love the Lord will fall but get right back up.

Yes, Theodore Roosevelt had it right. The credit does belong to the man or woman who is in the arena. The person who strives valiantly. Who sometimes knows high achievement and sometimes fails but still dares greatly.

Moms and dads who yell, "Nice try" in the stands also have it right. My apologies for thinking otherwise. Your voices from the bleachers can take solace in the fact that you're in good company with James, Paul, Solomon…and Teddy Roosevelt.

Checking the List

While trying and failing is not such an awful experience, the undeniable goal is still victory. You gotta love 1 Corinthians 9:24. "Do you not know that in a race all the runners run, but only one gets the prize? Run in such a way as to get the prize."

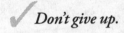 *Don't give up.*

Talk to Me

Except for the selected Scripture quotations, you really don't have to believe anything in this book. It's written by a flawed human author speculating on 52 items God may or may not include on a fictional bucket list.

That's why this chapter is so important. The next three pages point you back to a one-on-one relationship with the one absolute trustworthy source of all truth. That's right. Believe it or not, the Creator of the universe wants to talk you.

Look at the life of Jesus, and you'll get a clear picture of the importance of praying. Jesus modeled prayer throughout the Gospels. He prayed alone.

> Very early in the morning, while it was still dark, Jesus got up, left the house and went off to a solitary place, where he prayed (Mark 1:35).

He prayed for hours at a time.

> One of those days Jesus went out to a mountainside to pray, and spent the night praying to God (Luke 6:12).

He prayed with gratitude.

Then Jesus took the loaves, gave thanks to God, and distributed them to the people. Afterward he did the same with the fish. And they all ate as much as they wanted (John 6:11 NLT).

He prayed expecting miracles.

So they took away the stone. Then Jesus looked up and said, "Father, I thank you that you have heard me. I knew that you always hear me, but I said this for the benefit of the people standing here, that they may believe that you sent me."

When he had said this, Jesus called in a loud voice, "Lazarus, come out!" The dead man came out, his hands and feet wrapped with strips of linen, and a cloth around his face (John 11:41-44).

In the Garden of Gethsemane, Jesus also demonstrated how to pray in desperate times—even though he was fully aware that his prayer would not be answered in the way he hoped.

He withdrew about a stone's throw beyond them, knelt down and prayed, "Father, if you are willing, take this cup from me; yet not my will, but yours be done." An angel from heaven appeared to him and strengthened him. And being in anguish, he prayed more earnestly, and his sweat was like drops of blood falling to the ground (Luke 22:41-44).

Do you pray regularly? Or is prayer an item that wasn't even considered for your personal bucket list? Maybe you don't pray because you've never been properly instructed. Truthfully, you don't have to kneel, fold your hands, or close your eyes. (You can if it helps.) You don't have to speak in Latin, Greek, or gibberish. You don't have to memorize anything either.

If Jesus's example is not enough, you'll be glad to know that he also left clear instructions on how to communicate with the Almighty. In Matthew 6:9, Jesus says, "This then, is how you should pray."

What comes next is commonly referred to as the Lord's Prayer. In the New International Version, it's only 66 words (with the disputed ending), but not surprisingly, it covers everything you really need to consider when praying to God. Biblical scholars have spent countless hours considering the meaning of each phrase, but let's see what we can glean in just a page or so.

Our Father in heaven. The Creator of the universe wants a relationship with each of us. He's real. And he's living in a place of eternal glory. He sent Jesus to earth. He sent the Holy Spirit to live within us. God's home is heaven.

Hallowed be your name. Even God's name is set apart. Holy. Just mentioning his name unleashes unstoppable power.

Your kingdom come, your will be done. Those are true statements. God reigns. God's will triumphs. But they are also prayer requests. We are asking God to send his Son back for his triumphant return. Soon. And we are surrendering our will for his. He knows what's best for us anyway.

On earth as it is in heaven. These are two different places. But God is in control of both. Humans can't even begin to understand how the world and universe work. There's no way we can grasp the awesomeness of heaven.

Give us today our daily bread. This is pretty straightforward. Except it's not just bread. And it's not just daily. God supplies all our needs. From oxygen to sunlight to the way our brain turns squiggly lines printed on the pages of this book into ideas on how to know his will. How it all works together is God's gift to us.

And forgive us our debts, as we also have forgiven our debtors. This could be considered the centerpiece of the gospel. We must acknowledge our brokenness and ask for God's forgiveness. It's the blood of Christ that washes away our sins. If we understand the critical nature and power of forgiveness, we will also follow God's example. But our job is easier. All we have to do is forgive those who have wronged us one person at a time. We can't begin to compare that to God's promise to forgive all the sins of all the people throughout history who believe and trust in him.

And lead us not into temptation, but deliver us from the evil one. To be clear, God would never lead us into temptation. But he did give us free will, which means he *allows* us to be tempted, so we need to ask him to save us from ourselves. The second part pinpoints the urgency. Satan is real. And we can't face him alone.

For yours is the kingdom and the power and the glory forever. We've come full circle now. He's our Father in heaven, and his glory will last forever. He is the Alpha and the Omega.

Amen. Amen.

If you really want to know God's customized, 100 percent accurate bucket list for your life, you'll want to unwrap the gift of prayer. Turn to it often. When it becomes a regular part of your life, you'll discover a new clarity and confidence when making decisions. You may even surprise yourself when prayer becomes not something you do, but something you are. I believe that's what the Bible means when it says, "Pray without ceasing" (1 Thessalonians 5:17 NASB).

Checking the List

If you really want a more effective prayer life, pray for one. In other words, just pray.[8]

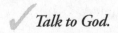 *Talk to God.*

32

Dodge Counterfeit Happiness

Caffeine is not my friend. I sit here at 1:26 a.m. not because I am inspired to write, but because I had one of those boxed apple pies from McDonald's and washed it down with a half cup of coffee at 7:45 p.m. A half cup. That's enough to keep my eyes from closing five hours and 41 minutes later. I should know better. I do know better.

On the other hand, every morning—including tomorrow morning—if I don't get a cup of joe by 10 a.m., a sweet little headache kicks in, beginning in the front of my forehead and then wrapping around my temples and settling like a dull ache about an inch inside my skull.

Please do not feel sorry for me. (You don't, I know.) This addiction or withdrawal or intolerance for caffeine is self-inflicted. And it's probably even curable. I wouldn't want to go cold turkey, but I could probably cut back little by little until I didn't need the caffeine hit quite so desperately every morning. And I certainly know better than to take even a sip of coffee or drink a half can of Coke after 4 p.m.

I am pretty sure all of us have some kind of self-inflicted addiction that we think brings us pleasure or competence or joy. But in truth, it brings minor amounts of pain and certainly drains a portion of the energy, productivity, hope, and happiness right out of our lives. Traditionally, we think of addictions as the overwhelming physical desires for things we would eat, drink, smoke, snort, or inject, such as caffeine, nicotine, opiates, amphetamines, marijuana, alcohol, sugar, chocolate, salty snacks, and energy drinks. For certain members of my family, that would include coffee, Peeps, ChapStick, and Tostitos with a hint of lime.

I'm straying way out of my area of expertise, but recent studies suggest that we humans can also be addicted to experiences that do not require ingestion of a food or drug. You won't be surprised to discover that we can be physically addicted to the Internet, television, sex, porn, gambling, video games, exercise, and even shopping. You need to know these habits and preferences go beyond emotional attachment. These behavioral addictions probably don't come with severe withdrawal symptoms associated with chemical abuse, but the cravings and compulsions can be just as real.

Claiming victory over any addiction requires more counsel than I can possibly offer in this short chapter. Thankfully, there are pastors, counselors, and doctors who are trained in this area. Not surprisingly, the Word of God also has much to say on the topic. First, know that you're not alone. Everyone is tempted. And with God's help, every temptation can be resisted.

> No temptation has overtaken you except what is common to mankind. And God is faithful; he will not let you be tempted beyond what you can bear. But when you are tempted, he will also provide a way out so that you can endure it (1 Corinthians 10:13).

One of the best strategies to fleeing temptation is to alter your behavior. Don't go places that remind you of old habits. The break room where you lit up. The pub where you once kept a growing bar tab. The route home from work that goes right past that ice cream shop or gambling arcade. The newsstand that carries those tempting magazines. Choose behavior that reflects the new you.

> Let us behave decently, as in the daytime, not in carousing and drunkenness, not in sexual immorality and debauchery, not in dissension and jealousy. Rather, clothe yourselves

with the Lord Jesus Christ, and do not think about how to gratify the desires of the flesh (Romans 13:13-14).

And just as there are behaviors to change and places to avoid, there are also individuals who drag you down. If they are true friends, then one plan of action is get yourself right so you can help them with their own recovery. But if their motivations are evil, then you know what you have to do.

> I urge you, brothers and sisters, to watch out for those who cause divisions and put obstacles in your way that are contrary to the teaching you have learned. Keep away from them (Romans 16:17).

The most important thing to remember is that you can't break an addiction on your own. You can try, but the demons don't give up that easily. That's why instructions like this are so critical to heed.

> Call on me in the day of trouble; I will deliver you, and you will honor me (Psalm 50:15).

Notice that once God delivers you from your crisis, he's expecting a response. That is, give him the glory. Which is usually pretty easy for most men and women who have hit bottom and found rescue in God's forgiveness and healing grace.

And hey. If this chapter hit you right between the eyes, track me down. I'd be honored to pray for you.

Checking the List

Don't settle for temporary, counterfeit happiness. Confess your addiction to someone who cares. Ask for a brutally honest response, and you may be on your way to a new life with real joy and greater purpose than you've experienced in a long time.

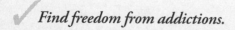 *Find freedom from addictions.*

Attend a Wild Game Night

I live in the western suburbs of Chicago. A couple winters ago, I drove seven hours due north, through the entire state of Wisconsin, to the Upper Peninsula and spent a weekend at Cornerstone Church in Ramsay, Michigan, population 400. I had a blast and was honored to hang out with the pastor, his family, and the faithful congregation.

That Friday night, I spoke at a wild game dinner in a church basement full of real men. The menu was fish, fowl, and beasts harvested and lovingly prepared especially for the occasion. Saturday morning, Pastor Todd and I spent two hours snowmobiling through wooded trails (and sometimes making our own trails). Near the end of our ride, across a frozen lake, I finally found the guts to open it up, topping 60 mph. That's pretty fearless for someone who had not been on a snowmobile since high school. At weekend services, I delivered a three-part message to teens, wives, and husbands.

I confess the entire experience was a bit of a culture shock. Not because it was the north woods. Not because I had never before tasted elk, quail, walleye, or bear. Not because of the friendliness or openness of the church members. The culture shock was that a small church 250 miles from any major city, with a full-time staff of two, was doing so much for others locally and across the planet.

The economy of the area had taken a real hit in recent years. Many church members had their share of personal challenges. But when Pastor Todd announced a new project working with the Voice of the Martyrs, it was met with enthusiasm. When it was time to pray for specific requests, the needs of others were clearly a priority. When I expressed some of my own burdens, I was surrounded with heartfelt prayer.

The vibrant people of Cornerstone Christian Church would teach this old dog a lesson. Or two. Or three. You see, I drove seven hours north with some preconceived notions.

Having spent most of my Sunday mornings worshipping in larger congregations, I somehow got the idea that bigger was better.

Having worked on fundraising projects for a variety of international ministries, I somehow had the idea that attendees at larger churches had deeper pockets.

Having produced radio programs with bestselling authors and highly regarded speakers, I somehow got the idea that men and women with well-known names somehow had cornered the market on delivering God's truth.

But bigger isn't necessarily better. God doesn't need spacious auditoriums. Spiritual impact cannot be measured by the number of music stands and amplifiers used by the worship team. Smoke machines and lasers are not required in every church. And God often does great things through modest beginnings. Jesus even described the kingdom of God as "a mustard seed, which is the smallest of all seeds on earth. Yet when planted, it grows and becomes the largest of all garden plants" (Mark 4:31-32).

Believe it or not, you can't put a dollar figure on generosity. Jesus watched a poor widow put two small pennies in the collection plate and stunned his disciples when he told them, "Truly I tell you, this poor widow has put more into the treasury than all the others" (Mark

12:43). Let me be clear—the Voice of the Martyrs was wonderfully blessed by the generous financial gift of this humble congregation.

Integrity, biblical authority, generosity, and high-impact truth-telling were alive and well at Cornerstone. Not just with the pastor but also his family and everyone else I met. They were inspiring examples of how to live out Galatians 6:2—"Carry each other's burdens, and in this way you will fulfill the law of Christ."

So don't settle for a church that bores you and makes you boring. Don't settle for worshipping with your hands in your pockets. Don't even bother getting up Sunday morning if your church experience doesn't challenge you to be more Christlike. The goal is to love your church.

However. That doesn't mean you have to go church hopping or shopping. Maybe God planted you right where you are to be part of something bigger than you could ever imagine. The formula for doing church right can be found in Acts 2:42-47.

> They devoted themselves to the apostles' teaching and to fellowship, to the breaking of bread and to prayer. Everyone was filled with awe at the many wonders and signs performed by the apostles. All the believers were together and had everything in common. They sold property and possessions to give to anyone who had need. Every day they continued to meet together in the temple courts. They broke bread in their homes and ate together with glad and sincere hearts, praising God and enjoying the favor of all the people. And the Lord added to their number daily those who were being saved.

Start this very day. Break bread. Pray. Worship. Give. Praise. Enjoy fellowship. Reach out. Revival might be right around the corner, right there in your home church.

Checking the List

Your bucket list should definitely include being an active member of a faith community that gives more than it receives. You can be sure you'll receive more than you can imagine.

 Experience love and worship in a sacrificial faith community.

Harvest the Fruit

In chapter 5, you were challenged to do some prolonged, thoughtful reconsideration of the Ten Commandments. The assertion was that those ten statements could very well be the perfect rules for living a complete and joy-filled life. You have to admit that rejecting idols, telling the truth, being faithful to your spouse, and the other seven commandments are worthy goals. Maybe even worthy of a bucket list.

Well, did you do it? Did you go back and read that list from Exodus 20 and really consider the subtext of each of those laws carved in stone? If not, do it now. Go ahead, I'll wait.

Okay then. In many ways, the New Testament has an even more intriguing list. Not a list of rules. Not specific things to do or refrain from doing. If you have surrendered your life to Christ, the list actually describes nine delightful character traits already at home in your heart. It's the fruit of the Spirit—love, joy, peace, patience, kindness, goodness, faithfulness, gentleness, and self-control—delivered as promised.

At the Last Supper, Jesus patiently explains the earth-changing events about to unfold over the following three days. Imagine the disciples' puzzlement when Jesus reveals that he is going to the Father but will send "another advocate" (John 14:16). Another advocate? How could anyone possibly replace Jesus, their living, breathing, walking friend who taught them and guided them with such clarity? Jesus calmed their fears and eased their grief:

> Very truly I tell you, it is for your good that I am going away. Unless I go away, the Advocate will not come to you; but if I go, I will send him to you. When he comes, he will prove the world to be in the wrong about sin and righteousness and judgment (John 16:7-8).

Sure enough, the second chapter of Acts records the coming of the Holy Spirit at Pentecost, and Christians have been blessed by his supernatural guidance ever since. As believers, if we stay connected to the vine—Jesus—we will bear fruit as promised.

> I am the vine; you are the branches. If you remain in me and I in you, you will bear much fruit; apart from me you can do nothing (John 15:5).

Those nine character traits are not arbitrary. They paint a complete picture of a man or woman living in harmony with all three members of the Trinity. Guided by the Holy Spirit, pursuing a life as modeled by Christ, and giving glory to the Father.

- *Love*—living with an open heart, fully engaged and equipped to love and be loved.
- *Joy*—being a witness to God's plan. Telling others what God has done in your life.
- *Peace*—trusting in God's sovereignty. Knowing his will shall be done.
- *Patience*—strength and endurance for all things. Waiting expectantly for Jesus's return.
- *Kindness*—serving with gentleness and respect. Putting others first.

- *Goodness*—truth-telling in the face of evil. Holiness that sets you apart.

- *Faithfulness*—seeking God's will. Praying without end.

- *Gentleness*—persevering against adversity. Turning the other cheek.

- *Self-control*—acknowledging the power of fleshly desires. Standing firm.

Spiritual gifts are given to individuals and revealed over time. On the other hand, the fruit of the Spirit are included in the DNA of every new believer. When we practice and nurture these virtues, they grow and bring new life to us and all those we meet.

Checking the List

Every authentic Christian is guided every moment of every day by the indwelling Holy Spirit. As our Advocate, he helps us recognize right and wrong, convicts us when we fall short, and empowers us to act boldly in the face of injustice. The Spirit is on duty this very moment. It's just that some of us choose not to follow his counsel.

 Nurture the fruit of the Holy Spirit.

Keep the Opposite of a To-Do List

D o you keep a list of things to do on your desk, in your smart-
phone, or posted on your fridge? This is different from a bucket
list. The things on your to-do list are very likely to be burdens, not
blessings. Running across that list is an almost guaranteed downer.

Let's say you're having a nice, productive day. Or you're cruising
through an extended fulfilling season of life during which you've discovered some simple joys. Blue jeans that fit. Credit cards mostly paid
off. A cell phone plan that fits your budget and needs. A few good
friends you can hang out with once in a while but not too often.

But then you notice that brutally long to-do list, and it smacks you
back to reality.

On the list are six or eight things that need to be done sooner rather
than later. Some have fast-approaching deadlines. Even worse, some
have no specific deadlines, but if you continue to ignore them, some
problems are just going to get worse and worse. Whether a to-do list
exists physically or just rolls around in the back of your brain, it has a
slight air of failure attached to it. The list includes broken things that
need fixing. Things that require time, energy, and resources you don't
have. Tasks that by definition, you have been incapable of completing.

The only pleasant thing about any to-do list is the moment when you can pick up a pencil and actually cross off something. Except that's usually about the time three more projects rise to the surface and are added to the list.

So let's do the opposite.

With pen and paper, make a list of things you have overcome in your life. Not things you have achieved, but minor and major challenges you have faced and defeated. Start by listing personal shortcomings or weaknesses that may have vexed you for a while but no longer stand in your way. Crummy stuff that is no longer crummy. Frustrating stuff that is no longer frustrating. This list is for your eyes only, so you can be totally honest.

To get you started, I'll list a few of my own shortcomings I'm not too embarrassed to reveal. I'm short. I have bad knees. I grew up with an older brother who was smarter, more worldly, and physically stronger than me. I never learned to diagram a sentence. I grew up with a speech impediment. I never set foot on an airplane until after I was married. I was afraid of hardball pitching. I occasionally choke under pressure.

You get the idea. I wasn't handicapped by a long list of severe limitations. But there were some things, albeit minor, that I had to face with honesty and overcome with specific action.

Some items on the list went away naturally over time. For instance, a man's vertically challenged stature isn't quite as important once you get out of high school. As my world expanded, I began to realize that height has nothing to do with intelligence or determination. And maybe short people have to work a little harder to get noticed, which means we learn to assert ourselves at a younger age. And that's not a bad thing.

Time also helped me appreciate my intimidating older brother. In my twenties, I even learned to applaud Mark's accomplishments. Instead of living in his shadow, I did my thing and he did his. I found myself actually feeling a sense of pride in having him as a brother.

For years, I wrapped my bad knees with ace bandages as a way to focus and prepare mentally for a wrestling match. Later, I simply accepted the fact that everyone has some physical limits and bad knees were mine. I was never destined to be a lifelong competitive athlete anyway.

To make up for my poor grammar training through my formative years, I taught myself to write in shorter, snappier sentences—that is, except for this one, which goes on and on and on, serving to prove my point; besides, my editors and readers like my use of short sentences. Don't you?

Chapter 22 documents how I overcame my speech difficulty. Worth mentioning again is how that unexpected gift of instantly improved pronunciation gave me the confidence to pursue opportunities onstage, in radio, and at podiums.

My bride and I took our first plane ride together on our honeymoon, which instantly turned that negative into a positive.

Being afraid of getting beaned by a baseball and sometimes getting the jitters when the game is on the line gave me empathy as a father and coach. Recalling my own shortcomings became motivation to do the necessary research and be intentional about guiding and encouraging my kids and others so they steer clear of the same frustrations. For example, I regularly told my kids, "Watching you, it's amazing how you get better in clutch situations. I used to choke. But when the game is on the line, you're the right person for the job." I'm taking no credit for my kids' achievements. But there's a special pride that comes when your children do stuff you couldn't.

Of course, I have many more shortcomings. And the items on my to-do list will never be completely crossed off. But I would suggest that on God's bucket list is this idea. Before you get overwhelmed by things you have to do, pause and look back at how far you've come.

Checking the List

How far have you come? Yes, we need to press on. We should not rest on our accomplishments. And sometimes we need to intentionally let go of the past. But we should always remember who we are as brothers and sisters of Christ. It's not a contradiction when Paul reminds us in Ephesians 5:8 that we should never forget how far we've come. "For you were once darkness, but now you are light in the Lord. Live as children of light."

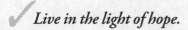 *Live in the light of hope.*

Run with Scissors

I was one of those good kids. Not goody-goody. Not the teacher's pet. Not the kind you wanted to smack because they tattled or carried a briefcase to school. I just never really got into any trouble.

But I'm also not ashamed to admit that I pulled a few pranks in my day. I really can't say much more than that. Before going public, I would have to track down the other perpetrators and get their permission to talk about what we did and where we did it. Since I lost track of them years ago, that just won't be possible. I'll just let your imagination take over and then quickly insist that it wasn't a big deal really. Nothing mean, illegal, or immoral.

My five kids were also good citizens and role models. And continue to be. But in the years since they were in high school, as we've sat around the kitchen table, once in a while a story never previously revealed will spill out that will have Rita and me laughing until it hurts. It's a blessing, really. Alec, Randall, Max, Isaac, or Rae Anne will recall an inspired moment from years ago that eventually led to some shenanigans. If we had known at the time, Rita and I would have had to deliver a short lecture or admonition. That's what parents do. But looking back...no harm, no foul.

Again, don't let your imagination run too far. But trust me that the laughs in recent years were totally worth the slight bit of mayhem back in the day.

Now, what does God say about all this? For sure, God knows our heart, our mind, and our actions, and we will be punished or rewarded accordingly. Jeremiah 17:10 reminds us, "I the LORD search the heart and examine the mind, to reward each person according to their conduct, according to what their deeds deserve."

God knows our motivations and shortcomings, so he readily acknowledges that he designed young people to sometimes push the limits of right and wrong. Proverbs 22:15 confirms, "Folly is bound up in the heart of a child."

Ecclesiastes 11:9 (NLT) even seems to give teenagers and children permission to go a little crazy. But make sure you read the entire verse: "Young people, it's wonderful to be young! Enjoy every minute of it. Do everything you want to do; take it all in. But remember that you must give an account to God for everything you do."

I take all of this to mean that sometimes, especially in our younger days, God expects us to get into some mischief. To do stuff with the singular purposes of making friends laugh. After all, Ecclesiastes does say there is a time for everything, including "a time to weep and a time to laugh, a time to mourn and a time to dance" (3:4).

Maybe we should do something our mommy told us never to do (of course, with appropriate boundaries). Something that even our daddy said was too dangerous. Something like…oh, I dunno…running with scissors.

Sound too daring for you? That's not surprising. Most of us have been told since we were four years old not to run with scissors. We've also been told that swallowing watermelon seeds is death defying. If you cross your eyes, they'll stay that way. And you must never, ever go swimming until an hour after you eat.

Every day we seem to have more rules and more laws. Some seem arbitrary. Some seem like overkill. Some feel as if they are just begging to be broken. Their only purpose seems to be to put roadblocks in the way of experiencing the world the way God created it. Don't climb too high. Don't talk to strangers. Don't put that bug in your mouth. But you know what? Mountains need to be climbed. Strangers need friends. In many cultures, bugs are a healthy snack.

At this point, my lawyers have advised me to remind all readers that this short chapter does not encourage or permit any reader to make illegal U-turns, tear tags off mattresses, steal packets of artificial sweetener from restaurants, text in a movie theater, or ignore the laws of your local, state, or federal government.

Now, if you already run with scissors, knock over outhouses, and bend most of the rules you meet, then clean up your act, for crying out loud. But if you're a Goody Two-Shoes in constant fear of tarnishing your reputation, then I've got some news for you. Your reputation needs some scuff marks. You're imperfect anyway, so you might as well act like it.

So whatever your age, I recommend you call up one of your slightly rowdy friends and plan a day of adventurous, good-natured mischief. You may want to consider cow tipping, loosening the tops of saltshakers at your favorite coffee shop, talking loudly in the library, calling the zoo and asking to speak to Mr. Lyon, or tying a hundred helium balloons to a lawn chair and cruising the neighborhood treetops.

Absolutely, obey all of God's rules. Feel free to bend all the others.

Checking the List

Just to clarify. The goal is to reflect God's glory in your life. To find joy in the day-to-day interactions with friends and family. You want a nonbeliever to look at you and say, "I want more of what they have."

Finally, if you're going through a miserable season of life, this may be the most important chapter in the book. I urge you to ask God for some joy. In John 16, Jesus promises his disciples, "I will see you again and you will rejoice, and no one will take away your joy" (verse 22). He goes on to say, "Until now you have not asked for anything in my name. Ask and you will receive, and your joy will be complete" (verse 24).

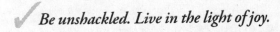 *Be unshackled. Live in the light of joy.*

Advocate Science

Are you surprised to hear that Christian colleges have science departments? Of course you're not. Science is an invaluable tool that brings about stunning and worthwhile advancements in physics, chemistry, computer technology, biology, genetics, architecture, meteorology, medicine, zoology, botany, ecology, and so on. The more we know about how the world works, the closer we get to knowing how God's design fits together.

Are you surprised to hear that most Christian colleges also have classes and professors who dig deeply into archaeology? You shouldn't be. Archaeology and its companion studies—paleontology and anthropology—are dedicated to finding the truth, just like all the other sciences. And isn't that what we all want? No one wants to be a fool. No one wants to live a lie. Truth is good. God is truth. And truth is what God wants us to pursue with every breath we take. Jeremiah 29:13 quotes God saying, "You will seek me and find me when you seek me with all your heart." I take that as a command to be a thinking Christian.

There's a rumor going around that those who follow Christ have somehow rejected every kind of science. The claim is that anyone who stands up for the Bible is a cotton-headed ninny muggins regarding the big bang theory, evolution, vaccinations, human sexuality, when human life begins in the womb, and a bunch of other controversial topics.

I'm not here to argue any angle of any of those debates. Drop me a line or collar me at a retreat, speaking engagement, or book signing. I'll be glad to share my thoughts on these topics.

I *am* here to challenge all Christians—not just university students—to keep seeking truth. Never be afraid of knowledge. And speak with confidence. That's what Jesus told his disciples to do.

> Bear testimony to me. But make up your mind not to worry beforehand how you will defend yourselves. For I will give you words and wisdom that none of your adversaries will be able to resist or contradict (Luke 21:13-15).

As an aside, I need to say that I'm offended when some doofus with a head full of hairspray claims to speak for all Christians or pretends to represent my side of a debate. Too often, I've seen ill-informed people prattle on with poorly conceived notions and simplistic logic. The result is dozens more cynics and atheists concluding all Christians are ignorant chumps. As I consider both sides, I'm not sure where my anger should be directed. At the bonehead claiming to represent all believers or the pessimists who suddenly think they know what I believe.

Please continue to take a stand and give testimony to how God is working in your life. But do your homework early and often. Better to say, "I don't know" than to make claims or statements that give ammunition to your adversary. As the fifth-century philosopher Augustine said, "He only errs who thinks he knows what he does not know."

Science is not a threat to Christianity. On the other hand, the greatest threat to seeking truth and sharing our faith might be the current trend toward deconstructionism, which suggests there is no such thing as truth. The best way to counter such a position is probably to cite personal experience. Make a statement that cannot be debated, such as "There is a new freedom and hopefulness in my life. And I believe it's a gift from God." It happened to you. And it's what you believe. They can call you a chump if they want, but they can't say you're wrong.

The Bible, of course, provides excellent instruction on personal evangelism. "Always be prepared to give an answer to everyone who asks you to give the reason for the hope that you have. But do this with gentleness and respect" (1 Peter 3:15).

Finally, even in your scientific pursuits, never forget love. Love confounds your average scientist. It cannot be defined in human terms. It cannot be measured. Love really cannot be questioned, debated, or solved. Which is perfectly fine. Because some things *cannot* be fully understood, and scientists *do* get things wrong sometimes. At a point in time, scientists told us the world was flat. The Titanic was unsinkable. Tobacco cured a variety of ills. The earth was the center of the universe. Wrong, wrong, wrong, and wrong. But 1 Corinthians 13:8 guarantees, "Love never fails."

Checking the List

You don't have to be the smartest person in the room. Instead, be the most humble. The most curious. The most caring. The most real. Be the one who listens and asks questions. Be the one whom other people approach when they want to talk about things that matter.

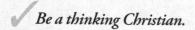 *Be a thinking Christian.*

Ask to Play Football

Without really discussing it with me, Rita began to brainwash our sons at an early age. When Alec was about four, she started cheerfully listing all the wonderful things he would do as he grew older. "Play baseball, read adventure stories, play the piano…" But then she would add, "And of course, you're not going to ride a motorcycle, box, or play football." As a young mom, she was just trying to protect her boys.

As for me, encouraging my sons not to pursue motorcycle riding or boxing made a certain amount of sense. The admonition against football was a gray area, and I didn't give it much thought. I had played football my freshman year of high school, and my performance was less than stellar. The coach put me in three games for a total of eight or nine plays.

Alec, who loved his mom, went right along with her sincere and frequent admonitions.

The shame, of course, is that Alec may have been our most athletic child. He hit six feet his junior year and had excellent speed and the confidence and courage of a champion. But sticking to the promises to his mom, Alec never played organized football.

Our second-oldest son watched this scenario with interest. Randy didn't get quite as brainwashed as Alec and somehow got the itch to play football. By sixth grade, Randy had played enough backyard and street football that it seemed like a natural fit. That's when he did an amazing thing. With humility and respect, he approached Rita and said, "I know you said we couldn't play football, so I'm giving you a year to think about it. When I get into middle school, I'd like to give it a try."

We had four boys by that time. They all wrestled competitively and had experienced plenty of nonfatal bruises and bashes on local soccer fields. And by this time, Rita had overcome most of her new-mom jitters, so she granted Randy's request. At the time, I don't remember Alec complaining about fairness. By then, he was finding personal fulfillment in other activities, including music, baseball, and youth group. Randy made his mark in football in middle school, stuck with it, and earned the spot as starting wide receiver his senior year in high school. A few years later, Max and Isaac also earned varsity letters. Max was team captain and MVP.

So you see, for his own sake and his little brothers', I'm glad Randy took that initiative. Football and other athletic endeavors have led to many rewarding milestones for our family. Participation in sports served us quite well.

Of course, this chapter is not about football. In a generation or two, football as we know it in America will be vastly changed. Or nonexistent. The NFL, youth sports, and traumatic head injuries are coming to an unavoidable crossroads. How that controversy unfolds is a debate for another venue.

In any case, despite the title of this chapter, no bucket list needs to include football. But *every* bucket list needs to include the skill demonstrated by 11-year-old Randy. That is, the ability to acknowledge authority figures and, with respect and submissiveness, present a thoughtful request for their consideration.

In the case of bringing our requests to God, that's just another reason to stay in constant communication with him. He wants us to ask thoughtfully, humbly, and persistently. God promises, if we put him first, he will make all our dreams come true. "Take delight in the LORD, and he will give you the desires of your heart" (Psalm 37:4).

If that's not working out for you, please check and recheck your motives. "When you ask, you do not receive, because you ask with wrong motives, that you may spend what you get on your pleasures" (James 4:3).

Once again, we can be sure God knows exactly what we need and is always watching out for our best interest. Scripture includes hundreds of verses on the topic of prayer, but the definitive teaching on how to bring a request to God might be found in the Gospel of Luke, shortly following Jesus's presentation of the Lord's Prayer.

> So I say to you: Ask and it will be given to you; seek and you will find; knock and the door will be opened to you. For everyone who asks receives; the one who seeks finds; and to the one who knocks, the door will be opened.
>
> Which of you fathers, if your son asks for a fish, will give him a snake instead? Or if he asks for an egg, will give him a scorpion? (Luke 11:9-12).

Whether he knew it or not, young Randy's request to his mother had all the characteristics of a solid prayer request.

So let's call this chapter a twofer. Your bucket list needs to include (1) the conviction to bring your deepest desires to God and (2) the humility to approach Mom—or any other authority figure—and ask for something that's important to you.

Checking the List

If you really want something, submit yourself to the appropriate authority with respect and a humble heart. Your parents, your boss, your teacher, God. *Go and ask.* Sure, you may not have all the information. Larger issues may overrule your petition. But if your intentions are honorable and your request sincere, the answer should usually be yes.

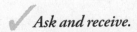 *Ask and receive.*

Go Beyond Golden

You know the golden rule, right? It's in Luke 6:31—"Do to others as you would have them do to you." You can find it with a slight variation in Matthew 7:12. And a similar concept appears in Romans 13:9 and Galatians 5:14—"Love your neighbor as yourself" (an Old Testament quote from Leviticus 19:18).

Like so much of Scripture, this is just plain good advice. Common sense for all people. As a matter of fact, you may have heard the claim that all the world's major religions have some version of the Golden Rule someplace in their sacred writings. Some people even argue that because the Golden Rule seems to be universal, all religions must be the same. Well, let's refute that faulty logic right now with four pretty obvious assertions.

First, if you search through other religious writings, you'll find passages that include something similar to the Golden Rule, but it's stated negatively.

- Confucianism says, "Do not do to others what you would not like yourself" (Analect 12:2).

- Buddhism says, "Hurt not others in ways that you yourself would find hurtful" (Udana-Varga 5:18).

- Hinduism says, "One should never do that to another which one regards as injurious to one's own self" (Anusasana Parva 113:8).

In other words, these religions are much more concerned with what their followers should *not* do than what they *should* do. Jesus's challenge to Christians, "Love your neighbor," is quite a bit different from saying, "Don't be mean to your neighbor." Jesus was all about proactive love. Healing, praying, feeding, instructing, correcting, gathering the children, and accepting the way of the cross. That's loving and doing positively for the sake of all humankind.

Second, stated positively or negatively, the golden rule is not particularly innovative. It's simply common sense and does not require divine inspiration. Being kind (or not being mean) is a smart strategy for life, but it isn't a particularly impressive spiritual feat. For example, being nice to your boss increases the chance for a promotion. Being nice to your kid's soccer coach may increase Junior's playing time. Being nice at a fast-food restaurant decreases the chance servers spit in your milkshake. The Bible even confirms the universal logic of the golden rule. A few verses down in Luke's Gospel, Jesus reminds us, "If you do good to those who are good to you," don't think of yourself as a hero. "Even sinners do that" (Luke 6:33).

Third, the Christian version of the golden rule doesn't just stop with loving your neighbor or doing good to others. Jesus's challenge takes this idea a giant step further. We're called to love not only our neighbors or others but even our enemies—and to "do good to them" (Luke 6:35). Loving our adversaries or being good to those who wish us harm is a little tougher, isn't it? But that's what Jesus expects of his followers.

Fourth, the biblical challenge gets even more difficult because we all like to get credit for the good things we do.

> When you give to the needy, do not let your left hand know what your right hand is doing, so that your giving may be

in secret. Then your Father, who sees what is done in secret, will reward you (Matthew 6:3-4).

That's right. Do your good work in secret. For sure, you'll be rewarded, but not by our worldly culture. In some cases, you won't receive your reward until you're home in heaven.

Indeed, the golden rule is nice. But before you sharpen your pencil to check off that item on God's bucket list for you, please check your motives. Love means having your neighbor's best interest in mind. Love needs to extend to all—even your enemies. And you might even try doing awesome, loving deeds in secret.

Checking the List

Ever hear someone say, "All religions are the same. They all have the Golden Rule"? Next time, respond by saying, "The Golden Rule is easy—for the most part it's self-serving. I suggest you try reading and living the rest of the gospel."

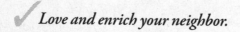 *Love and enrich your neighbor.*

Be a Friend

How many friends do you have? True friends?

I daresay that most people have had fewer than a dozen authentic friends over the course of their life. Perhaps even less than five. To make my point, my intention was to begin this chapter by recounting the first names of the small number of individuals whom I consider to have been true friends over the years. Then on second thought, I realized doing such a thing so publicly might require just a bit too much soul-searching. May I simply say, ladies and gentlemen, you know who you are.

Actually, the Bible suggests that limiting the number of friends you have might be a good thing and that true friends are a blessing. "A man of too many friends comes to ruin, but there is a friend who sticks closer than a brother" (Proverbs 18:24 NASB).

So, can you name your friends who are closer than a sibling? A working definition of friendship might be in order. But let's move beyond the dictionary.

- "A true friend unbosoms freely, advises justly, assists readily, adventures boldly, takes all patiently, defends courageously, and continues a friend unchangeably" (William Penn, 1644–1718).

- "Friends are helpful not only because they will listen to us, but because they will laugh at us; through them we learn a little objectivity, a little modesty, a little courtesy; we learn the rules of life and become better players of the game" (Will Durant, 1885–1981).

- "To give and receive advice—the former with freedom and yet without bitterness, the latter with patience and without irritation—is peculiarly appropriate to genuine friendship" (Cicero, 107–44 BC).

True friendship is rare because it requires more than time and proximity. It takes more than just hanging out. According to Penn, Durant, and Cicero, friendship requires trust, honesty, and vulnerability.

In the Old Testament, we find those traits in the famous friendship between David and Jonathan. Saul passed over his own son, Jonathan, and named David to be the next king. Still, that didn't place a wedge of envy or entitlement between them. Both men responded with humility and integrity.

The book of Ruth recalls the friendship that grew between a mother-in-law and daughter-in-law, Naomi and Ruth. Together they suffered loss and traveled cross-country as widows. The two women stayed committed to each other and exchanged advice. That Old Testament book ends with a genealogy showing that Ruth became the great-grandmother of David.

Then there are friendships that didn't work out quite so well. In the book of Job, when Satan is allowed to destroy Job's family, fortune, and health, the frustrated man is visited by three so-called friends. Their original intentions may have been compassionate, but the men demonstrated very little wisdom, loyalty, or empathy for Job, admonishing him with all the wrong explanations for his suffering. Those three men weren't friends at all!

The very first verse in the book of Psalms warns about being friends with anyone who ridicules or turns their back on God. "Blessed is the one who does not walk in step with the wicked or stand in the way that sinners take or sit in the company of mockers."

Friendship, even when it's difficult, has long-term rewards and is well worth including on your bucket list. Friends trust each other enough to share and receive wisdom, advice, and correction with respect and humor. Friends share your joy and lighten your burdens.

Friendship opens the door to mutual accountability. Iron sharpening iron. Just as one friend can honestly say, "Watch your tongue," the other should be enabled to say, "Watch your temper." Spoken in private, intimate words of gentle correction, appraisal, and admonition are received well. That's how friendship works.

Checking the List

In addition to trust, honesty, and vulnerability, Jesus helped define friendship through the ideals of love and sacrifice. "Greater love has no one than this, that one lay down his life for his friends" (John 15:13 NASB). He is the living example of such love. And that truth still applies to his followers today.

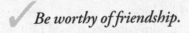 *Be worthy of friendship.*

Be Ready to Die

Kara Tippetts, a Colorado pastor's wife and mother of four, started the blog *Mundane Faithfulness* to share simple truths about motherhood and living in kindness. After being diagnosed with cancer, Kara's posts began to dig a little deeper, revealing to the world what it's like to truly, deeply, and joyously love Jesus. Her blog content moved beyond the ordinary—beyond mundane faithfulness—to reflect the courage, honesty, and sense of humor of a beautiful young mom preparing to leave her family and meet God.

Hundreds of thousands of lives have been touched by Kara's words in her blog and her book, *The Hardest Peace*. Journals and blogs that document personal battles with terminal illness are not in short supply, but this one is different. In photo after photo, the smiling faces of Kara and her family are almost impossible to reconcile with their daily reality. Her words graciously reflect self-awareness but not an ounce of self-pity. The cancer and death sentence seem to have delivered Kara from petty concerns, holding grudges, and small talk.

One of Kara's final posts before her death in March 2015 reveals an honest appreciation for her upcoming journey in the shadow of Psalm 39:4—"Show me, Lord, my life's end and the number of my days; let me know how fleeting my life is."

My little body has grown tired of battle, and treatment is no longer helping. But what I see, what I know, what I have is Jesus. He has still given me breath, and with it I pray I would live well and fade well. By degrees doing both, living and dying, as I have moments left to live. I get to draw my people close, kiss them and tenderly speak love over their lives. I get to pray into eternity my hopes and fears for the moments of my loves. I get to laugh and cry and wonder over Heaven. I do not feel like I have the courage for this journey, but I have Jesus—and He will provide. He has given me so much to be grateful for, and that gratitude, that wondering over His love, will cover us all. And it will carry us—carry us in ways we cannot comprehend.[9]

"What I have is Jesus…I get to pray into eternity…He will provide…We cannot comprehend." Kara's words reflect an understanding of our relationship with God.

In humility, Kara described the origins of her story as mundane. I don't buy that. Yes, God used her cancer to take her story to a deeper level and a broader audience. You and I probably wouldn't know about that Colorado pastor's wife if tragedy had not entered her life. But her final three years on earth were exceedingly beautiful and worthwhile only because she laid a foundation of love and kindness in advance. It's worth emphasizing that Kara did not "find religion" after the diagnosis. Getting cancer to reveal her need for a Savior was not on Kara's bucket list. She was ready to die well before any symptoms showed up. That is not mundane.

Kara has given us the privilege of seeing someone die the right way. Which happened only because she chose first to live the right way. Kara knew death was coming. And she was ready. Are you?

Checking the List

There are all kinds of takeaways from the story of a life lived well but taken too soon. Make today count. Be grateful for this moment. Speak in love. Reserve your spot in heaven. Be ready.

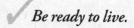 *Be ready to live.*

Arm Yourself for Mockers

Consider this chapter a public service to Christians who are tired of being mocked.

Do you sometimes feel attacked by late-night talk shows or animated sitcoms? Do those metal fish decals with little feet and the word "Darwin" tick you off?

Maybe you're tired of the new atheists claiming that science is on their side. At a rally a few years ago in Washington, DC, bestselling author Richard Dawkins instructed some 20,000 people to "ridicule and show contempt" for religious people and their doctrines.

If you're feeling weary of such attacks—or maybe even starting to be swayed by them—keep reading. When it comes to the topics of Jesus Christ, God, and the Bible, many of the smartest people and deepest thinkers who have ever lived were quite clear in their beliefs.

*One drop of Christ's blood is worth
more than heaven and earth.*

—Martin Luther

*The greatest act of faith takes place when a
man finally decides that he is not God.*

—Johann Wolfgang von Goethe

People travel to wonder at the height of mountains,
at the huge waves of the sea, at the vast compass of
the ocean, at the circular motion of the stars, and
they pass themselves by without wondering.

—AUGUSTINE

The worst moment for the atheist is when he is
really thankful and has nobody to thank.

—DANTE GABRIEL ROSSETTI

The real attitude of sin in the heart towards God is
that of being without God; it is pride, the worship of
myself, that is the great atheistic fact in human life.

—OSWALD CHAMBERS

I believe in Christianity as I believe that the sun has risen,
not only because I see it, but because by it I see everything else.

—C.S. LEWIS

He is no fool who gives what he cannot
keep to gain what he cannot lose.

—JIM ELLIOT

I've read the last page of the Bible. It's
all going to turn out all right.

—BILLY GRAHAM

Men occasionally stumble over the truth, but most of them
pick themselves up and hurry off, as if nothing had happened.

—WINSTON CHURCHILL

It ain't those parts of the Bible that I can't understand
that bother me, it is the parts that I do understand.

—MARK TWAIN

*Christianity is one beggar telling another
beggar where he found bread.*
—D.T. Niles

God is at home; it is we who have gone for a walk.
—Meister Eckhart

*Sir, my concern is not whether God is on our side; my greatest
concern is to be on God's side, for God is always right.*
—Abraham Lincoln

*The nature of God is a circle of which the center is
everywhere and the circumference is nowhere.*
—Empedocles

A comprehended god is no god.
—John Chrysostom

*As sure as God puts his children in the furnace
he will be in the furnace with them.*
—Charles Spurgeon

He who has God finds he lacks nothing: God alone suffices.
—Teresa of Avila

*If God were small enough to be understood, he
would not be big enough to be worshipped.*
—Evelyn Underhill

*Out of 100 men, one will read the Bible, the
other 99 will read the Christian.*
—D.L. Moody

> *God exists whether or not men may choose to believe in*
> *Him. The reason why many people do not believe in God*
> *is not so much that it is intellectually impossible to believe*
> *in God, but because belief in God forces that thoughtful*
> *person to face the fact that he is accountable to such a God.*
> —ROBERT A. LAIDLAW

> *A heathen philosopher once asked a Christian,*
> *"Where is God?" The Christian answered, "Let*
> *me first ask you, Where is he not?"*
> —AARON ARROWSMITH

> *When we cease to worship God, we do not*
> *worship nothing, we worship anything.*
> —G.K. CHESTERTON

> *What comes into our minds when we think about*
> *God is the most important thing about us.*
> —A.W. TOZER

Feeling better about your convictions? Don't stop there. One of the most important tools to drop in our bucket list is our own reasoned thought. Let's commit to move beyond a few quotations from smart folks throughout history and be smart ourselves. Establish some core convictions that have personal application to your story. Prepare yourself to defend those beliefs as if your life depended on it. Knowing what and why we believe is the best way to prepare for the mockers.

Checking the List

Field reports from mission agencies and national news organizations document that thousands of Christians continue to be tortured and persecuted around the world. In comparison, I'm confident you can endure some occasional disparaging remarks by late-night comedians and cartoon characters. Also, you probably won't be physically assaulted by self-serving artists with a radical agenda. Still, at the Sermon on the Mount, Jesus delivered a promise to all those who follow Christ: "Blessed are you when people insult you, persecute you and falsely say all kinds of evil against you because of me" (Matthew 5:11). So...if you feel insulted, consider yourself blessed!

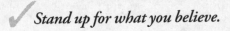 *Stand up for what you believe.*

Untangle the Conundrum of Nice People

I know you're a wonderfully kind and reasonable person. (Me too.) There are lots of wonderfully kind and reasonable people in this world. None of us are perfect. But during the course of a week, you will likely run into quite a few people who open doors for strangers, don't litter, use their turn signals properly, say "Pardon me" when they burp, and clean up the mess their doggie leaves in the park.

A certain percentage of those wonderfully kind and reasonable people are followers of Christ. They most likely pray, read the Bible, and go to church. They get up in the morning with a sense of purpose. They live with a joy and peace almost too good to be true. And they go to bed secure in the knowledge they have a place reserved in eternity living with the Creator of the universe.

Others of those wonderfully kind and reasonable people think anyone who calls themselves a Christian is ignorant, gullible, and being conned out of their hard-earned money every Sunday morning when their church passes the collection plate.

I understand. And because I pick up my Bible once in a while, I'm not surprised. Through the centuries, there have been millions of people who weren't overtly evil, but simply believed God doesn't exist or Jesus was a fraud. They said the Bible is not God's inspired Word. And they believed this world is our one and only home. When we're dead, we're dead.

Again, we're not talking about the mockers and attackers from the previous chapter. We're talking about wonderfully kind and reasonable people. Teachers, doctors, bankers, barbers, postal workers, and store clerks. Neighbors and friends. Maybe some very good friends. You can have delightful and worthwhile conversations with these people about the weather, local politics, gas prices, and whether the Cubs will ever win the World Series.

But if you mention Jesus, they will smile politely and change the subject. After all, they are wonderfully kind and reasonable people. They are living reasonably happy lives, and they pretty much don't want to offend.

So what's the difference between Christians and non-Christians? Often they look and act the same. There's no physical difference. There's no birthright. There's no magic involved. But there is a difference.

At a moment in time, some of the wonderfully kind and reasonable people realized they needed a Savior and asked Jesus to take control of their life. That's when the two kinds of people we've been talking about headed in opposite directions. Some took the narrow road and some took the wide road, as described in Matthew 7:13-14.

> Enter through the narrow gate. For wide is the gate and
> broad is the road that leads to destruction, and many enter
> through it. But small is the gate and narrow the road that
> leads to life, and only a few find it.

The wonderfully kind and reasonable people who chose the narrow path received a bonus gift. Along with salvation they received the permanent gift of the Holy Spirit. Ephesians 1:13 confirms, "When you believed in Christ, he identified you as his own by giving you the Holy Spirit, whom he promised long ago" (NLT).

In our saga about the two types of wonderfully kind and reasonable people, here's where it gets a little sticky. For now, both groups are in the world. Both groups of wonderfully kind and reasonable people will keep doing their best, but both will make mistakes. As a matter of fact, you could find one individual who does believe in Christ who made a bunch of mistakes. And you could find one individual who rejected Christ who made fewer mistakes. How do you explain that?

Well, for one thing, those who have the Spirit are being convicted of their mistakes. They are more likely to know they messed up. Plus, as time goes on, the Holy Spirit will continue to sanctify them, reveal God's plan, and set them apart for good works.

Regretfully, the wonderfully kind and reasonable people who rejected Christ are left to maneuver this world under their own power. And not even wonderfully kind and reasonable people can keep that up forever.

Here in this world, good things and bad things happen to all people. That's fairly obvious, but Matthew 5:45 confirms, "He causes his sun to rise on the evil and the good, and sends rain on the righteous and the unrighteous." The difference is how people respond.

As we saw in an earlier chapter, those who accepted Christ and received the Spirit have an extra dose of love, joy, peace, patience, kindness, goodness, faithfulness, gentleness, and self-control. When the storms of life hit, they are better equipped to keep it together. With their eternal destiny secured, they also have a heavenly perspective and the confidence to move forward using those gifts to serve others.

Still, the question remains, what happens to the wonderfully kind and reasonable people who have not yet found the narrow door? God's plan is that some of the wonderfully kind and reasonable people who *do* know Christ will show them the way. Through the power and leading of the Holy Spirit. Are you up for that challenge?

Checking the List

I totally understand how wonderfully kind and reasonable agnostics sometimes get frustrated when they meet a sold-out follower of

Christ. They think, "What gives this person the right to judge me?" Or, "They're no better than me." And they're right! Everyone—even someone who is wonderfully kind and reasonable—falls short of God's perfect standards. The difference is that somehow the truth of the gospel found its way into the head and heart of believers. And they said yes.

 ***Trust the Holy Spirit.***

Be Your Brother's Keeper

Here's a story you already know. It's about a boy who was a first-born child. Actually, he was *the* firstborn child...ever.

Cain was the son of Adam and Eve. His mom and dad had tasted paradise and even walked with God, only to have lost the privilege. But whatever lesson they learned, they didn't pass it on to their eldest child. Cain became a farmer of sorts, working the soil. When he presented some of the fruits of his labor as an offering to God, they were rejected. And Cain became angry. What made it even more irritating for Cain was that God readily accepted a gift from his little brother, Abel. The Bible doesn't say specifically why Cain's gift wasn't worthy. But we get a hint when we read that Abel's gift was top-notch—the best of the first-born lambs from his flock. Maybe Cain skimped, not giving his best to God. Maybe his heart just wasn't in it.

Whatever the case, God speaks directly to Cain and gives some pretty clear instruction to him and the billions of people to come through the words of Genesis 4:6-7.

> Then the LORD said to Cain, "Why are you angry? Why is your face downcast? If you do what is right, will you not be accepted? But if you do not do what is right, sin is

crouching at your door; it desires to have you, but you must rule over it."

Of course, the Lord knew why Cain was angry and downcast. But it's not unusual for God to ask questions to which he already knows the answers. Just a chapter earlier he asked Adam and Eve, "Where are you?…Who told you that you were naked? Have you eaten from the tree that I commanded you not to eat from?" (Genesis 3:9,11). God wasn't expecting a response. He was well aware of what had already transpired with the fruit, the snake, and the tree of the knowledge of good and evil.

After his two initial questions to Cain, God gave some pretty clear instruction with implications for all mankind. In essence, he simply said, "Do what is right. Or else." The statement came with a warning and a confirmation that Cain was at a critical crossroads. But God left the decision up to Cain.

That tells us a few things worth remembering. There is right and wrong. It's not a mystery. We can know it. Plus, we have a choice. We need to choose what is right, and there are consequences if we don't! What's more, Genesis 4:7 tells us that sin is waiting to pounce but God has provided a way to face sin and claim victory.

We know what happened. Cain ignores the instruction, lures his little brother out to a field, commits the first murder, lies to God about Abel's whereabouts, loses the ability to grow crops, and is banished to wander the earth without God's immediate presence. Cain can't say he wasn't warned. Neither can we.

Checking the List

God gave Cain a couple opportunities to do the right thing and even included a warning in between. God knew that with each of Cain's bad decisions, sin would creep a little closer, ready to pounce. Cain was given a chance to step back and recalibrate, but he didn't. His first negative choice—probably trying to pass off a few second-rate vegetables as an offering—was really no big deal. But it opened the door to the next sin—murder. The story of Cain and Abel is another example of the slippery slope. How one sin leads to another.[10]

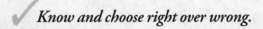 *Know and choose right over wrong.*

Celebrate Quirks

Just about every time Rita gets the mail, she leaves the mailbox open. For years that wretched, evil habit ticked me off.

I hinted, suggested, encouraged, and begged her to close the mailbox after retrieving the mail. I would forcefully slam the lid on the mailbox with a resounding clang, especially if she was within earshot. My frustration over her horribly irresponsible behavior sometimes lasted well into the evening. I could count on Rita's mailbox insensitivities negatively impacting my personal happiness every afternoon. Except for Sundays and national holidays.

Do I exaggerate? Perhaps a little. But only to make a point.

My bride is awesome. She is beautiful, intelligent, warm, thoughtful, and loving. It is stunning how often we are in sync. We are on the same page when it comes to almost all controversial life issues, including where to live, how many kids to have, how to raise them, spiritual beliefs, and vacation plans. Just about every time I think of her, I smile. But that mailbox habit really fried my burger. That was my perfect wife's one deficiency. That tragic flaw stood in the way of my personal unconditional contentment.

Do you see the absurdity of my fury? It took me a while, but I finally came to my senses. And I laughed out loud. Finally, that mailbox— open or closed—became a symbol of how grateful I was God had given me a bride who wonderfully and completely matched my needs. Now every time I see her quirk exposed, I celebrate. She's my wife, and I love everything about her, including her quirky refusal to close the mailbox.

By the way, I also am not quirk-free. Allow me to confess. I stir Rita's pots. I sing in the car. I leave dishes in the sink. I steal her favorite pillow. I require a certain kind of pen to sign greeting cards. I guess the next line of dialogue in movies right out loud (only at home, not in theatres). I won't play Monopoly if I can't be the wheelbarrow. I brush my teeth in the shower. I point out misspelled words.

These quirks are not very appealing, and some of them could be downright appalling to my bride. I probably should ask, but I won't. To her credit, she has not attacked me regarding any of them. When I'm dead and gone, I hope Rita will miss my many and varied charming eccentricities.

All that to say, if someone you care about exhibits a quirk (not a dangerous, mean, or thoughtless habit), just let it go. Shrug it off. Hang tough. Bear with it. "Be completely humble and gentle; be patient, bearing with one another in love" (Ephesians 4:2).

For the noble-minded reader, consider taking it a step further. Don't just tolerate or endure the quirk. *Cover it with love.* "Above all, love each other deeply, because love covers over a multitude of sins" (1 Peter 4:8). If a relationship is suffering from a divisive quirk—yours or theirs— you have the power to turn the foible into something endearing. Love can do that. Love can take a harmless quirk or a sin that needs correction and turn it into a blessing. Something that was divisive now brings unity.

Finally, the principle applies to more than just one-on-one relationships. On God's bucket list is the reminder that all of humanity has quirks, shortcomings, and infirmities. God has no favorites. He sees all we are and still loves us. "There is neither Jew nor Gentile, neither slave nor free, nor is there male and female, for you are all one in Christ Jesus" (Galatians 3:28).

So whatever differentiates you from the person across the street or on the other side of the planet, it's worth remembering that we're all flawed, broken, and in desperate need of a handyman.

I think most of us already knew that, right?

Checking the List

Do you catch yourself being quick to judge? Consider the story of the woman caught in adultery. The self-righteous crowd was a little too bloodthirsty and eager to judge the woman. With quiet authority, Jesus suggested they first examine their own lives. He said, "Let any one of you who is without sin be the first to throw a stone at her" (John 8:7). With those words hanging in the air, the crowd dispersed.

Worth noting: Jesus didn't just tell the woman she could leave. He gave her an assignment—"Go now and leave your life of sin." Which suggests we should all try to be more aware of our own quirks and consider eliminating them. Each time we look within ourselves, we get a chance to see a few more items on God's bucket list for our lives.

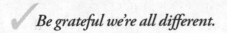 *Be grateful we're all different.*

Recognize Jesus

A few years ago, a young man in a baseball cap positioned himself in a Washington, DC, Metro station and began to play his violin for the hundreds of commuters during the morning rush. In 43 minutes, fewer than a dozen people stopped to listen, and exactly $32.17 in loose change and small bills were tossed in his violin case. What almost no one realized was that the young man was virtuoso Joshua Bell playing a Stradivarius worth $3.5 million. Just a few days earlier he had filled Boston Symphony Hall, where seats averaged more than $100.

If you were in that Metro station that day, please don't feel embarrassed. I'm sure the violin melodies dancing through the normal cacophony of the morning rush were exquisite. But when you're not looking for something, you rarely find it. Recognizing anyone—even a master virtuoso—is especially difficult when you're caught up in your own tunnel vision of hustling to work and prepping yourself for a productive day.

Even most of the folks who recognized Mr. Bell probably didn't stop for more than a moment. Some commuters probably saw him, did a double take, wondered what was going on, and then continued on with their day.

The Gospels record several instances in which individuals from all walks of life came face-to-face with Jesus. Those moments of recognition changed their lives forever.

In Luke 2, senior citizens Simeon and Anna immediately welcome the new baby Jesus. Prophecies and the Holy Spirit had told them they would see the Messiah. Simeon quite accurately said, "This child is destined to cause the falling and rising of many in Israel" (Luke 2:34).

The Samaritan woman at the well initially considered Jesus to be a prophet because he exposed her sinful lifestyle. Soon her eyes were fully opened to whom she was talking with. "Leaving her water jar, the woman went back to the town and said to the people, 'Come, see a man who told me everything I ever did. Could this be the Messiah?'" (John 4:28-29).

Matthew 27:54 records what happened immediately after Jesus's death on the cross. "When the centurion and those with him who were guarding Jesus saw the earthquake and all that had happened, they were terrified, and exclaimed, 'Surely he was the Son of God!'"

On that first Easter, two disciples walking the seven miles from Jerusalem to Emmaus were trying to make sense of the events of the weekend. Luke 24:15-16 describes what happened. "Jesus Himself approached and began traveling with them. But their eyes were prevented from recognizing Him" (NASB). Later, when Jesus broke bread with them, they suddenly recognized him, and he disappeared from their sight.

Thomas didn't believe the story of the resurrection until he met the risen Christ and saw the wounds of the crucifixion. "'My Lord and my God!' Thomas exclaimed. Then Jesus told him, 'You believe because you have seen me. Blessed are those who believe without seeing me'" (John 20:28-29 NLT).

Simeon, Anna, the woman at the well, the centurion at the foot of the cross, two disciples walking to Emmaus, and doubting Thomas all eventually saw Jesus and recognized him for who he is. And their lives were never the same.

God's bucket list for every person includes "Be ready to meet Jesus."

That could be after your life ends here on earth, or it could be at the second coming. The good news is that the events of Christ's return will be unmistakable. "At that time people will see the Son of Man coming in clouds with great power and glory" (Mark 13:26).

For sure, Jesus will not be wearing a baseball cap and playing the violin in a Metro station. All of humankind will hear shouts from angels and fanfare from trumpets. Believers in Christ who are dead will rise from their graves, and those still alive will be caught up in the clouds to meet Jesus.

All believers who ever lived will be reunited in the presence of God. Don't miss it.

Checking the List

There's really not a lot to do. Jesus has done all the heavy lifting. While many of the other items on God's bucket list are designed to help make the most of life on earth, this one is all about accessing heaven. You don't even have to visually recognize the dusty, parable-teaching Messiah of the first century. But you do need to follow the lead of the Samaritan woman, the centurion, and Thomas. Admit your sins. See him as the Son of God. And accept him as Lord of your life.

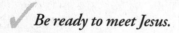 *Be ready to meet Jesus.*

47

Seek Wise Counsel

When I was 25, my sister informed me that Rita and I were buying a house. I believe her exact words were, "You're buying a house."

Mary Kay knew what she was talking about. Five years older than me, she had already established herself as one of the shining stars of the real estate community in the Fox Valley. She took great joy in finding the right house with the right-sized mortgage for first-time home buyers. Word of mouth spread among young families looking for starter homes. As their incomes and families grew, couples came back to Mary Kay when they wanted to trade up to gain a master bath, extra bedrooms, or a bigger yard. When their children grew up, Mary Kay also found just the right house for that next generation. Even later, she'd help empty nesters downsize or cash in so they could retire to a warmer climate or move closer to grandkids.

I'm not sure if Mary Kay mapped out her decades-long career with great intentionality. But I do know she placed great value on integrity and trust.

Rita and I were smart enough to take her advice (which, by the way, sounded a lot like a command). At the time we had one son and another on the way. At a family gathering, Mary Kay casually asked what we were paying for rent on our townhome. Like only big sisters can, she told us exactly what we were about to do. Three months later we were homeowners.

Really, it was great advice. Sure, we stretched our budget. It was a humble starter house with three small bedrooms and one bathroom. The only shower was in the basement and more than a little grotty. During our first chilly winter, the north wind whistled its way through our clapboard siding. But we were homeowners. Two and a half years later, we sold that starter home for a profit of $20,000 and got a great deal on a new house in a new subdivision. That second house also had Mary Kay's blessing.

When it came to residential real estate, we got wise advice from a person we could trust. And that's worth its weight in gold.

It took a while, but we did the same thing with our auto mechanic. After getting burned by more than a few con men, we finally found a mechanic we could absolutely trust. Over the years, Kevin of Kevin's Automotive has saved us a bundle by making repairs for half of what other shops quoted, looking over used cars before we made a purchase, and even sending us to other mechanics who could do certain jobs for a little less.

It pays to have a wise, experienced, and trustworthy realtor, auto mechanic, plumber, electrician, and accountant in your life you can count on. The Bible suggests we surround ourselves with people who know what they're talking about. "Plans fail for lack of counsel, but with many advisers they succeed" (Proverbs 15:22).

Wise counsel is especially critical when it comes to spiritual concerns and matters of personal integrity. After all, we're only human. Scripture passages can be misinterpreted and taken out of context. We can claim to hear God's calling when it's really our own greed, lust, or envy that's driving a decision. We might make a decision that's good for business but bad for our conscience.

Do you have a small group or accountability partner you can turn to? Someone to help you apply Scripture and interpret prayer? People you can trust to hold your feet to the fire and open your eyes to what's really going on? It's a definite item for your bucket list.

Meeting with your small group or accountability partner should generally not be a painful experience. It's mostly about sharing knowledge and encouraging growth. But it's also about asking tough questions.

"Any angry outbursts since we last met?"

"How are your credit card balances?"

"How's your prayer time?"

"How many days since we last met have you spent at least 15 minutes in the Bible?"

"Did you call Taylor and ask for forgiveness yet?"

These kinds of questions may sound a little threatening. But your accountability partner or small group leader isn't really asking the questions. You are. You have given them permission to hold you accountable. And it works. If you're open and vulnerable, you will soon take great strides in becoming the person God wants you to be. You'll be checking off more bucket-list items than you could ever do on your own.

God made people for relationship. Relationship with him and with others. That's how we become our best selves—meeting, challenging, motivating. Hebrews 10:24-25 says it well. "Let us think of ways to motivate one another to acts of love and good works. And let us not neglect our meeting together, as some people do, but encourage one another, especially now that the day of his return is drawing near" (NLT).

Don't process important life decisions alone. For the well-being of your family, bank account, conscience, and soul, seek wise counsel at every turn. You'll still make mistakes, but you'll have people right there who care and who will help you pick up the pieces and learn from your experience.

Finally, if you have wisdom to share, don't keep it to yourself. Someone in your life needs *your* counsel, love, and helping hand.

Checking the List

When you surround yourself with wise advisers, the collective wisdom is far greater than any one individual has alone. And your failures will be less catastrophic because your partners will also share some of the burden. Even Jesus had a small circle of people he could trust.

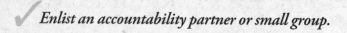 *Enlist an accountability partner or small group.*

Know the Pythagorean Theorem

Like most students, you probably learned the Pythagorean theorem in seventh or eighth grade and promptly forgot it the following summer. You may recall that it has something to do with how the two short sides of a triangle relate to the longer side. You may even hazily remember the formula $a^2 + b^2 = c^2$.

When I was in middle school, I was just catching on to the Pythagorean theorem when my family sat down to watch the annual broadcast of *The Wizard of Oz*. (This is before VCRs, back when families sat together and watched broadcast television as it was being broadcast.) As I watched one of the final scenes in the 1939 MGM classic, something struck me as inaccurate.

While rescuing Dorothy, the Scarecrow had displayed innovation and street smarts which, according to the Wizard, earned him an honorary diploma. When the quartet arrived back in the Emerald City, the scriptwriter needed to demonstrate how the character in search of a brain had suddenly realized his immense intellect. In the scene, the Scarecrow receives the faux diploma, points to the side of his head, and rapidly rattles off a faux Pythagorean theorem. This is exactly what actor Ray Bolger says: "The sum of the square roots of any two sides of an isosceles triangle is equal to the square root of the remaining side."

Well, that's really not even close. Any midlevel math student would tell you that the Pythagorean theorem applies to right triangles and not isosceles triangles, that the words "root" and "roots" don't belong, and that the variable must be the hypotenuse. Accurately stated, "The square of the hypotenuse of a right triangle is equal to the sum of the squares of the other two sides."

I assume the screenwriter had access to the proper wording of the ancient principle of geometry but the film crew's consensus was that it just didn't matter. Why fuss about whether Mr. Bolger says "isosceles" or "hypotenuse"? No one remembers the exact definition anyway. Besides, in the end, the Scarecrow didn't have to *be* smart, he only had to *appear* smart.

This is all very dangerous territory. I realize it's just a movie. And viewers had already suspended belief by hurtling over the rainbow, skipping with a scarecrow, and fleeing flying monkeys. But the 1939 filmmakers are suggesting that when it comes to something we know to be true, such as the Pythagorean theorem, accuracy doesn't matter.

However, accuracy does matter. Otherwise, chaos reigns. If the rails don't line up, train cars tip over. If the city inspector miscalculates, your tap water becomes poisonous. If God allows the earth to spin 2 percent slower, the oceans slosh into your backyard.

There is order to the universe. And we need to do what we can to keep order in our world.

Knowledge is the beginning of order. Railroad engineers know how to align and secure train tracks. Your local water department follows clear guidelines for treating and distributing water. God knew what he was doing when he hung the stars and spun the planets.

There is order. There is truth. We can know it. As a matter of fact, we must know it. As a 12-year-old, I knew the *Wizard of Oz* script was scientifically inaccurate because I knew the Pythagorean theorem. I compared fiction to truth.

As an adult, I can do the same thing. Our culture presents all kind of options—some helpful, some not so helpful. How can we know the truth? The answer is simply stated but takes a lifetime to apply. God has revealed truth in the Bible, and it's our job to know it and apply it to our lives. Yes, we'll make mistakes. But that doesn't mean we shouldn't try.

Need examples? Exodus 20:13-15 teaches we shouldn't murder, commit adultery, or steal. Deuteronomy 15:7-8 teaches we should be generous to the less fortunate. Matthew 7:1-5 teaches we should not be self-righteous or hypocritical. Romans 13:1 teaches we should respect government authority. Matthew 6:14-15 teaches we should be eager to forgive others.

The truth we all seek is found in the Bible. Without it, we're setting ourselves up for serious judgment. In Matthew 22, the Sadducees tried to trap Jesus with a question about heaven. That led to a warning: "You are in error because you do not know the Scriptures or the power of God" (verse 29).

Acts 17:11 describes how those who sought truth were "of more noble character...for they received the message with great eagerness and examined the Scriptures every day to see if what Paul said was true."

Is knowing the great truths of mathematical theory on God's bucket list? Probably not. But God does place a high value on knowing and living according to the truth of the Bible.

In summary, if you're attempting to state the Pythagorean theorem, accuracy is achievable. If you're trying to live your best life, a trustworthy and accurate plan is written down for you. Grab your Bible and dig in using your brain, heart, and courage.

Checking the List

The Bible shouldn't be intimidating. It should be comforting. We can live without speculation. We can know right from wrong. We can know truth. And by the way, the Scriptures may be thousands of years old, but they still apply. "All your words are true; all your righteous laws are eternal" (Psalm 119:160).

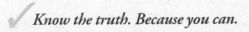 *Know the truth. Because you can.*

Give Credit Where Credit Is Due

Sometimes when the boss chews you out, it goes in one ear and out the other. But this time I knew my creative director, Rudy, was absolutely right, and it forever changed the way I made presentations and spoke in meetings.

It was downtown Chicago on Michigan Avenue at the ad agency then called Campbell Mithun. Jerry was my creative partner, and he and I were presenting storyboards to the account team for a new commercial for Kroger supermarkets. As was typical back then, the art director would stand and describe the visual aspects of each panel, and then the copywriter would come forward to walk the small audience through music cues, sound effects, and any dialogue or voice-over narration.

Developing the concept, script, and visuals and making the presentation were all a collaborative effort. But that day, instead of using the word "we," I used the word "I." Several times. Jerry, as usual, did an outstanding job describing the visual aspect of the proposed commercial. A heroic, animated pair of scissors would chase an evil dollar sign through a three-dimensional landscape of household products and food packages. Our goal was to create a memorable personality for Kroger's iconic cost-cutter scissors.

Unfortunately, when I took my place to describe our custom music, sound effects, and narration, I sounded as if the entire spot was my idea. That wasn't my intention. In fact, the overarching idea for the innovative chase sequence had been Jerry's. Everyone loved the spot. We sold it to the client and even talked them into nudging up the budget for some special effects.

After the presentation, Rudy called me into his office and explained certain secrets of success for working in the creative department of a major ad agency. Things like sharing credit and honoring teammates. He specifically said to use the word "we" instead of "I" when presenting storyboards and layouts. It was the best kind of meeting. Short, truth-filled, and constructive.

My old boss's two points stuck with me: Sharing recognition is the best way to get ahead. And two heads are better than one. Whether he knew it or not, Rudy was right in line with Scripture.

- "For all those who exalt themselves will be humbled, and those who humble themselves will be exalted" (Luke 14:11).

- "Two are better than one, because they have a good return for their labor" (Ecclesiastes 4:9).

Giving credit where credit is due is an excellent strategy in business. It's an even better strategy in life. Let's even call it a mandatory addition to God's bucket list for our lives.

In the fifth chapter of Matthew, you'll find Jesus launching his public ministry with the famed Sermon on the Mount. It begins with the Beatitudes and continues with a couple verses in which Jesus tells us to be salt and light to the world. Then comes verse 16. This sentence just might be a formula for life, our reason for being on the planet: "Let your light shine before others, that they may see your good deeds and glorify your Father in heaven."

There's a lot in those 19 words, so read them again. Jesus is saying don't be shy. Let your light shine. Do great things. Live and act in such a way that people look at you and say, "Wow," "Nice job," or even, "You're my hero." That's when you graciously give credit where it belongs. Identify yourself as a Christian and reveal that your motivation is to give back to God. To give him glory. By doing that, you will be illuminating a path that helps lead others out of the darkness so they, too, can glorify God.

Let's close this chapter with three questions.

- Who or what is your motivation to shine bright and do great things?
- Do your work colleagues, classmates, close friends, casual acquaintances, and neighbors know your motivation?
- Finally, when you earn kudos for a job well done, who gets the glory?

Thanks, Jerry, for your creative partnership so many years ago. Thanks, Rudy, for telling it like it is.

Checking the List

If we do good works without acknowledging whom we serve, we get the glory ourselves. That's not a good plan.

So maybe we should be more outspoken about identifying ourselves as Christians. Maybe we should take ethical stands at work. Maybe we should be known for reading our Bible at lunch. Maybe we should be more vocal about justice and morality in our schools and community. Maybe we should have a fish on our car.

Of course, you know the problem. As soon as you identify yourself as a Christian, the stakes go way up. Your good works will glorify God. Your not-so-good works may give others one more reason to say, "Christians are all hypocrites." Yikes.

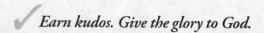 *Earn kudos. Give the glory to God.*

Do the Right Thing

Here in our final chapters you may be starting to feel as if God's bucket list is a little overwhelming. Like a bucket that's overflowing with responsibilities. Sorry. That was never the intention, but it was pretty much unavoidable.

Once you begin digging into Scripture, the truths keep coming. There's so much we need to take in and ponder. It's all good stuff—useful guidance for life.

> All Scripture is inspired by God and is useful to teach us what is true and to make us realize what is wrong in our lives. It corrects us when we are wrong and teaches us to do what is right (2 Timothy 3:16 NLT).

That's good news, right? These first 50 chapters or so may have helped open your eyes to valuable insights you had not previously considered. Rules to remember. Concepts to embrace. Clear direction.

Well, I hate to break it to you, but you've been duped. Scammed. Double-crossed. Because you know what? *You are now responsible to follow through and do the right thing.*

Before cracking open this book, you may have been blissfully ignorant about loving your enemies or nurturing the fruit of the Spirit. The Ten Commandments were old and irrelevant. Angels were imaginary.

Bible study and defending your faith were things that only preachers and scholars needed to do.

Well, now you're on the hook. You are responsible for following through and making good use of all the items on the list we've been compiling. James 4:17 (NLT) tells you something you may not want to hear: "It is sin to know what you ought to do and then not do it."

That's right. Sin is not just intentionally doing wrong. It's also knowing the right thing to do and intentionally not doing it. Sound harsh? Maybe a little. But you have to agree it makes great sense.

Please don't regret picking up this book. The act of checking off items on God's bucket list for you is ultimately an extraordinarily positive experience. Do the right thing…and the long-term result is guaranteed glorious.

Got it?

Still feel on the hook? Allow me to take off just a little bit of that pressure. You're human, which means you will still be making a mistake once in a while. Your less than perfect choices will actually cause you some frustration. Which is a good sign! As the Holy Spirit nudges, you should hate the sin in your life.

> I don't really understand myself, for I want to do what is right, but I don't do it. Instead, I do what I hate. But if I know that what I am doing is wrong, this shows that I agree that the law is good. So I am not the one doing wrong; it is sin living in me that does it (Romans 7:15-17 NLT).

That passage from Romans doesn't excuse your behavior or thoughts. It simply confirms that you continue to be a sinner in need of a Savior. You are a lawbreaker who hates the fact that you sometimes forget or ignore the law.

Please don't beat yourself up. But do take regular inventory and be ready to apply the brakes. As soon as you realize that you've messed up, stop and admit it. When you find yourself heading down the wrong path, stop and do a U-turn before you really get lost.

To clarify, this book and this author are not passing judgment. God is. Likewise, you shouldn't expect or allow your friends and family to hold you accountable for your sins. You are accountable only to the One who created you.

Worth mentioning: One of the reasons he needs you to make right choices is that your actions impact others. Don't be a stumbling block.

> Yes, each of us will give a personal account to God. So let's stop condemning each other. Decide instead to live in such a way that you will not cause another believer to stumble and fall (Romans 14:12-13 NLT).

So...now that you know the right choices to make, start making them! Not because you're afraid of the repercussions. Not for the rewards. Rather, do it as service to God. Do it as an ambassador of his kingdom for the sake of everyone God puts in your pathway.

Checking the List

Only one person who ever lived did it perfectly. The rest of us have to live with the consequences of our not-so-good decisions. Thankfully, we have Jesus to model righteousness. The Holy Spirit to serve as our conscience. And the Father to forgive us when we come before him. When the dust settles on our life, that all means we can actually live without regrets.

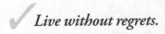 *Live without regrets.*

51

Write Your Tombstone

The topic is tombstones. And the question is, should thinking about what goes on your tombstone be on your bucket list? I totally understand if you want to leave all that up to your beloved family. But let's kick the idea around for a few pages anyway.

If you plan ahead, you can actually have pretty much anything you want carved on yours. Taphophiles—individuals with an abnormal interest in cemeteries—delight in the variety of ideas and images found in graveyards they explore. Whether overgrown or neatly maintained. Near the center of big cities or on the outskirts of small towns. With the feel of a sunny park or an eerie potter's field. When it comes to epitaphs, tombstone tourists confirm that anything goes.

Actually, Scripture verses are quite popular and may include the complete text or just the reference.

- "Whosoever believeth in him should not perish, but have eternal life" (John 3:15 KJV).

- "They can no longer die; for they are like the angels" (Luke 20:36).

- "The LORD is my shepherd; I shall not want" (Psalm 23 NASB).

- "Where, O death, is your victory? Where, O death, is your sting?" (1 Corinthians 15:55).

- "I am going there to prepare a place for you" (John 14:2).

- "I am the resurrection, and the life: he that believeth in me, though he were dead, yet shall he live" (John 11:25 KJV).

Personally, I may include "Psalm 127" on my memorial plaque. Not all 97 words, just the reference, which might encourage people who show up at my grave to actually open their Bibles and look it up for themselves. (Feel free to do that now.) As an aside, I'm also thinking I might want my grave marker to be level with the ground to make the grass easier to mow. Maybe I'll let my kids decide that.

When it comes to summarizing your life in granite, there are all kinds of options. My dad's stone includes his full name, dates, and the words "Loving Husband, Father and Papa." For the last 30 years of his life, everyone called him "Papa." He loved that role.

Other sentiments might include life mottoes or reminders to the living. Beyond "Rest in Peace," walk through any cemetery and find such sentiments as "Life is not forever—love is," "Until we meet again," and "Forever in our hearts." Keep walking and you also may find the morbidly amusing "I told you I was sick!" A cemetery in Thurmont, Maryland, features a stone that reads, "Here lies an atheist. All dressed up and no place to go." Makes you think.

Not surprisingly, celebrities often take more latitude in how they are memorialized. Statues, laser-cut images, and movie quotes can be spotted in cemeteries in and around Hollywood. Here are just a few examples of how these celebrities managed to have the last word...carved in stone:

- Mel Blanc, the voice of Bugs Bunny, Daffy Duck, and a thousand other animated characters, silently echoed the immortal words of Porky Pig, "That's all, folks!"

- The epitaph for Merv Griffin, television pioneer and talk-show host, promises, "I will not be right back after this message."

- The legendary film star of *Mr. Roberts, Some Like It Hot,* and *The Odd Couple* had just three words chiseled in his stone (which mimics a theatre marquee): "Jack Lemmon in."

- Jackie Gleason fittingly used one of his famous catch-phrases: "And away we go!"

- Rodney Dangerfield, the comic who got no respect, must have seen himself as not worthy of his final resting place. Below his name is carved, "There goes the neighborhood."

- Frank Sinatra's modest gravestone includes lyrics from one of his hits: "The best is yet to come."

The most relevant information on any gravestone may be the dates. Taphophiles, historians, and genealogists count on seeing a birth and death year on virtually every memorial stone. Biblically speaking, it's a smart idea to track those two dates and be well aware of the limits on the time we have. Psalm 90:12 offers a plan for how to live wisely, "Teach us to number our days, that we may gain a heart of wisdom."

In other words, don't worry so much about being clever on your tombstone. Instead, be wise with your days.

Checking the List

Once in a while, you do see a third date carved on a headstone. Bold followers of Christ sometimes include the date on which they were born again. Arguably, that life event is more important than the day you were born or the day you died. And that's the one date you can actually control. Memorializing in stone the date you received Christ would be an undeniable witness to family, friends, and anyone who strolls the grounds.

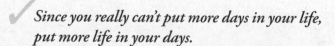 *Since you really can't put more days in your life, put more life in your days.*

Finish What You Start

I have a file folder in a file folder in a file folder on my computer desktop labeled "unfinished manuscripts." That's not a total embarrassment. I believe most authors have a similar folder. Mine contains the first chapter of a novel that will never be finished because I discovered I am not a novelist. It also contains a children's book in need of an illustrator. There's also a manuscript for a book titled "Dad Haiku," which will be completed as soon as I invest another 100 hours in writing fractured haikus. Click around that folder and you'll also find a few allegorical tales that I never finished because it came to my attention that publishers have no desire to publish allegorical tales. And anyone who knows me won't be surprised to hear there's a partial screenplay focusing on the theme of fathers, faith, and baseball.

All of the above, I started. All of the above, I have not yet advanced to a satisfactory conclusion. And that's okay, right?

Sometimes you get into a project and realize it's not your sweet spot. Or it's no longer necessary. Or your time is better spent elsewhere. Or the budget has dried up. Or it's going to take more work than you anticipated. Or the basement has flooded and needs your attention. Or you have a sore tummy. Or your favorite TV show is on. Or you just don't feel like it. Or maybe you're really just a lazy slug with no talent and no future.

Excuses are easy to come by. Just ask Rita. She's heard so many of my excuses that she's beginning to suspect my idea of a comfy, fully functioning home doesn't exactly match her idea of a comfy, fully functioning home. I can't blame her. I do tend to put off for tomorrow stuff she wants done today. Actually, I'm pretty sure some of the jobs on my honey-do list were written on the walls of our cave with woolly mammoth blood.

So, what projects have you left unfinished? Are you, too, a specialist in delay tactics?

It's true that we can't finish everything we start. But it's also true that finishing well has distinct benefits. As the apostle Paul neared the end of his life, he did not hesitate to confirm that even though there was much work still to do, he had done his part. "I have fought the good fight, I have finished the race, I have kept the faith" (2 Timothy 4:7).

What's more, there's a wonderful promise in 1 Corinthians 15:58 that God is going to make sure your work has eternal significance. "Brothers and sisters, stand firm. Let nothing move you. Always give yourselves fully to the work of the Lord, because you know that your labor in the Lord is not in vain."

Perhaps the best example of finishing with a flourish can be found in the well-known story of David and Goliath. When the story is told (especially to children), the tale begins with the young shepherd boy protecting his sheep and ends with the Philistine giant crashing to the ground after being hit by a smooth stone from David's sling. But that's not the end of that encounter. David, the future king, has to make sure the job is finished. First Samuel 17:51 describes the action. "David ran and stood over him. He took hold of the Philistine's sword and drew it from the sheath. After he killed him, he cut off his head with the sword." That's a good example of finishing the job. When the Philistine army saw Goliath's head roll, that's when they turned and ran.

Jesus's final words before his death on the cross were recorded in John 19:30. "Jesus said, 'It is finished.' With that, he bowed his head and gave up his spirit." In that moment, the atonement for the sins of the world was complete.

So back to your list of things to do. If it's your own personal bucket list, don't panic if some of those items are never finished. It's really not a tragedy if you never hit a hole in one or bake the perfect soufflé. Most people never get a single poem published or receive a single patent, trademark, or copyright. You might not ski the Alps or see a ballgame in all 30 major league parks. You might not swim with a stingray or run with the bulls. And that's all okay. Those things aren't critical to how God sees you.

But it would be a tragedy if you missed the top items on God's bucket list. All the previous chapters may be summed up in action points described in a few key verses.

- "Seek first his kingdom" (Matthew 6:33).
- "Commit your works to the LORD" (Proverbs 16:3 NASB).
- "I have been crucified with Christ and I no longer live, but Christ lives in me" (Galatians 2:20).
- "Go into all the world and preach the gospel to all creation" (Mark 16:15).
- "Whatever you do, do it all for the glory of God" (1 Corinthians 10:31).

While you're seeking God's kingdom, working for him, dying to self, preaching the gospel, and giving glory to God, feel free to pursue other cool and valuable stuff. Really, it's up to you. I totally recommend you begin lots and lots of amazing projects. I also hope you find a few that are worthy of your time, energy, and focus. Most of all, I pray you finish well.

(As I type the last words of this book, that's one more thing I can cross of my bucket list. Now it's your turn.)

Checking the List

It's not how you start. It's how you finish.

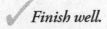 *Finish well.*

Notes

1. Cited in Randy Cassingham, *This Is True Weird News.* www.thisistrue.com.

2. "Maternal Deprivation Syndrome," Health Guide, *New York Times.* www.nytimes.com/health/guides/disease/maternal-deprivation-syndrome/overview.html.

3. Adapted from Jay Payleitner, *52 Things Kids Need from a Dad* (Eugene: Harvest House, 2010), pp. 101-4.

4. Adapted from Jay Payleitner, *52 Things to Pray for Your Kids* (Eugene: Harvest House, 2015), pp. 53-54.

5. Cited in "What could happen to you: tales of big lottery winners," NBC News, May 17, 2013. usnews.nbcnews.com/_news/2013/05/17/18323470-what-could-happen-to-you-tales-of-big-lottery-winners. Also cited in "Sudden lottery fortune no panacea," CNN, September 24, 2013. www.cnn.com/2013/09/20/us/lottery-windfall-disasters/.

6. John Barefoot et al., "Hostility, CHD Incidence, and Total Mortality: A 25-Year Follow-Up Study of 255 Physicians," *Psychosomatic Medicine* 45 (1983): 59-63. Cited in Norman E. Rosenthal, *The Emotional Revolution* (New York, NY: Citadel, 2003), p. 217.

7. Lynette Holloway, "In Schools, Family Tree Bends with Times," *New York Times*, February 7, 1999. www.nytimes.com/1999/02/07/nyregion/in-schools-family-tree-bends-with-times.html.

8. Adapted from Payleitner, *52 Things to Pray for Your Kids*, chapters 4 and 17.

9. "Homecoming," *Mundane Faithfulness* (blog), March 22, 2015. www.mundanefaithfulness.com/home/2015/3/22/homecoming.

10. Adapted from Jay Payleitner, *The One Year Life Verse Devotional* (Wheaton: Tyndale, 2007), p. 96. Used by permission of Tyndale House Publishers, Inc. All rights reserved.

More Great Harvest House Books by Jay Payleitner

The Dad Book

52 Things to Pray for
Your Kids

10 Conversations Kids
Need to Have with
Their Dad

365 Ways to Say
"I Love You"
to Your Kids

52 Things Kids Need
from a Dad

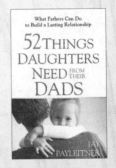

52 Things Daughters
Need from Their Dads

52 Things Sons Need
from Their Dads

52 Things Husbands
Need from Their Wives

52 Things Wives Need
from Their Husbands

To learn more about Harvest House books and
to read sample chapters, visit our website:

www.harvesthousepublishers.com

HARVEST HOUSE PUBLISHERS
EUGENE, OREGON